The Need to Weed

Devised and written by Valerie Ailes

Illustrated by Daphne Gander

(Front cover by Andrew Miller)

Published by Murphy Chemical Ltd

Acknowledgements

I would like to thank all the following people who have helped me in different ways to achieve this book. First, Bryan Hazlehurst of Murphy Chemical Ltd who initially encouraged me to put pen to paper and actually write the book. George Culpan of Murphy's Advisory Department who has been a mine of information and patiently answered my endless questions. My sister, Daphne Gander, whose superb colour illustrations really make the book come to life. Mr Alan Ailes for editing it. Mr R. Chancellor and Mrs Peta Simmons of the Weed Research Organisation who have helped me tremendously with the seedling section and supplied me with excellent references and information. Finally, Miss Sarah Gardner who has spent many hours typing (and re-typing!) my manuscript.

ISBN No. 0 9507435 0 X

©1981. Murphy Chemical Ltd. Wheathampstead, Herts.
Design, layout and typography by V. Ailes
Printed in England by Sir Joseph Causton & Sons (Eastleigh) Ltd.

Preface

I welcome this book as an invaluable aid to the identification and control of garden weeds, both in their seedling stages and in full growth. The names used are those recommended by the Botanical Society of the British Isles, but some alternative names are included.

There has been much progress in recent years in the development of garden weedkillers, and a wide range of products is now available to solve virtually all weed problems. However, the successful use of weedkillers relies considerably on accurate identification of the weeds to be treated in order that the most effective treatment can be applied.

Products from manufacturers other than Murphy Chemical have been included to give the best possible recommendations. Should you have any specific problems, the Murphy Advisory Department will be pleased to answer them. This service is free of charge, in exchange for a stamped addressed envelope, and any letters should be addressed to me at the address below.

Happy weeding!

George Culpan
Advisory Manager

Murphy Chemical Ltd
Wheathampstead, St Albans, Herts AL4 8QU
Tel (058 283) 2001

Footnote
This book has been compiled with the greatest of care and we believe that the information is accurate and the recommendations suitable for the purposes indicated. The book does not, however, take the place of the directions on the product label which should always be read in full before use.

Contents

Why I needed to weed!

Weeding can be one of the most harrowing experiences known to man. Apart from the sheer waste of time and effort involved, to all but the most experienced gardener, there is also the problem of what to remove.

Weed seedlings can appear extremely fit and healthy and emanate a promise of great blooms to come to the inexperienced eye! It was this factor which prompted the writing of this book. On purchasing our present house with its beautiful garden, we moved in at the height of the summer. The previous owners were expert gardeners and it had been their desire to hand the garden over at its peak. The lawns were like velvet, the rockeries ablaze with colour, roses and bedding plants bloomed with profusion—and all weed-free—an idyllic situation! At this point I should mention that both my husband and I were very keen to take on this beautiful garden, but were also totally inexperienced gardeners.

At first it was quite easy. We spent a lot of time gardening but it was mainly a caretaker's job, routine work keeping everything looking as we had inherited it. Autumn and winter came and passed—with us spending many a winter night ardently reading garden tomes, gleaning information. In the spring we duly followed precise instructions and made use of our newly acquired knowledge of pruning, trimming and basic preparation.

Gradually the garden came to life with buds and new foliage emerging everywhere. Inexperience and rose-tinted optimism led us to believe that as spring turned to summer and our first anniversary at the house approached, the garden would look as it did when we moved in. Well it did—basically! But what we had in addition was an absolute mass of completely uninvited guests—the weed brigade. I, in my wisdom, had watered and nurtured *all* new growth, imagining I was cultivating future begonias, chrysanthemums and camellias, *not* as I subsequently discovered, ground-elder, dandelions, thistles and almost every other floral infestation!

It was then that I wailed if only I could have identified all the weed seedlings and plants that in my ignorance I had aided to healthy growth, I would not have had this problem.

Hence my decision to research the subject and not be caught out again. Thanks to the immense help given to me by the advisory department at Murphy Chemical Ltd, and the Weed Research Organisation, I have been able to write this book, and I trust it will help and inform others like myself.

To war!

Everybody has a personal view about gardening. It can be the most important and absorbing interest in life, a pleasant pastime, a necessary chore or just a plain bore. Most people fall into the middle two categories, finding gardening both enjoyable and stimulating, but also totally frustrating at the same time! Enjoyment comes from the satisfaction of growing beautiful new life in flowers, fruit, shrubs and lawns and in actually seeing the results of one's labours. Frustration comes from that eternal menace—weeds—which forever seem set to appear from nowhere and rear their triumphant heads in sheer defiance at one's efforts to exterminate them!

This book has been written with the objective of helping you to fight and eradicate this common menace with as much success as possible. First by identifying most of the weeds you are likely to find in your garden, at both seedling and mature stage; and second by establishing each weed's identity and type, giving you the ammunition with which to fight the enemy.

Weed treatment-the methods

Weeds fall into two main categories. Annuals, which propagate themselves by seeding from the mature plant and which only last one year; and perennials, which spread by the roots and shoots creeping under or over the soil, and persisting from year to year. Perennials can also produce seeds to spread the infestation further afield.

Annual weeds are relatively easy to cope with if identified at an early stage: the perennials present more of a problem in that their roots are already well established. There is also a third, but less common type, the biennials. These form vegetative plants in the first year, and then flower and die in the second year.

The methods for treating and eradicating weeds, like many other things in life, have progressed and improved over the years. There are now many new chemical treatments available to help the gardener which will indeed save both time and trouble, but old and conventional methods must not be forgotten or ignored as they still have a vital role to play. Most of us bless the invention of the motor car and value its contribution to our modern lifestyle, but equally would not deny that there are many situations where it is both more sensible and practical to return to basics and walk!

This book concentrates mainly on the use of herbicides—or chemical weedkillers—as these now play a major role in gardening technique and have many advantages if used correctly and sensibly. However, I would like to mention here some other methods which should still be given consideration and used when appropriate.

Hand weeding

Still one of the best methods, but *only* if the entire root is removed. So often one tugs at a well-established weed only to find that it snaps off at some point when under stress, leaving half the root still well embedded in the soil (and out of sight!) and only the foliage and part of the stem in one's hand. This is obviously useless and a total waste of effort as the weed will rapidly re-establish itself and reappear. The time factor must also be considered with this method—a time and motion expert would, I'm sure, give it a very low rating! Another point which is often forgotten is the amount of good soil which is discarded along with the weed when this method is used. Over a period of years you could well throw away several hundredweights (or equivalent kilos!) of valuable tilth. However, in situations where a weed is growing very close to a wanted plant, be it in flower bed or vegetable row, this is often the ideal method.

Hoeing

An excellent method under certain conditions—that is where the tilth of the soil is good, and also when the weather is dry and will therefore finish the job by withering the weed once uprooted until it is dead. If it is damp the weed will survive and all you will have accomplished is the transplanting of your weeds to different positions, for they will merely re-establish themselves. The hoe is again ideal for clearing weeds in between vegetable rows and flower beds where hand weeding is impractical.

Mulching

This is a method by which a whole area of ground is physically covered by a substance, thus smothering the area, blocking out all light, and therefore making it almost impossible for any plant or weed to survive. Methods include using grass cuttings, peat, bark or sawdust to a depth of about three inches, but the modern method is the use of black polythene sheets. These are held down by either stones or earth and are very effective in preventing any germination beneath them. This method is of particular benefit in some types of vegetable areas and around such fruit crops as strawberries, where they can serve an extra purpose by keeping the fruit clean and deterring pests such as slugs. However, vast areas of black polythene will not enhance the appearance of your prize flower beds!

Flame guns

A rather drastic and Wyatt Earp approach whereby one uses a mechanical device to burn away offending foliage. This method has advantages where a dense, neglected area has to be cleared completely prior to re-cultivation, but should be used with extreme caution as it is totally indiscriminate and will burn everything within its radius.

Chemical weedkillers

Many people still tend to be extremely wary of using chemical weedkillers—or herbicides as they are commonly called. True, the traditional method in fiction of neatly bumping off one's spouse or mother-in-law has been to slip some arsenical weedkiller into the unsuspecting subject's cup of tea, and thus the idea of deadly poison has long been associated with the humble potting shed. However, a great deal of progress has been made in recent years on the formulation of less toxic chemicals to remove this danger, and there are now stringent government regulations regarding safety, to which manufacturers must conform before marketing a product to the public. However, it cannot be too strongly emphasised that one *must read and follow the instructions on each product very carefully*.

Trusting that any innate fears you may have had are now dispelled, let us tackle the problem of which weedkiller to buy. Once in a garden centre or shop, one is confronted with a myriad of choice in the form of numerous brand names packaged in assorted bottles, boxes, sprays and pots, and to the uninitiated, it may be difficult to choose the correct one for a particular job. However, looked at logically it is quite simple. There are only three basic types of weedkiller, "Contact", "Translocated", and "Residual", and each is chemically formulated to perform in a specific way.

These three types can be bought in both "selective" and "non-selective" forms, and although it may appear obvious, it is important to understand that a "selective" weedkiller will only kill certain types of plants in an area to which it is applied, whereas a "non-selective" weedkiller will kill *all* plant life it comes into contact with, even if by accident.

1. Contact weedkillers

Contact weedkillers are primarily used for the quick removal of short-rooted annual weeds, usually at seedling or immature stage. They are called "contact" weedkillers as they will kill any *foliage* with which they come into *direct* contact. They are applied to the leaves, stems and shoots of unwanted plants and work by direct scorching action, or by destroying the chlorophyll manufacturing system in the green tissue, thus stifling the ability to live. A treated plant soon turns brown, withers and dies.

Advantages

• Quick and efficient method of treating annual weeds at seedling and immature stage.

• Used as an overall application in "non-selective" form they will quickly clear a weed-infested area.

• Used in a "selective" form they can be used on lawns to destroy offending weeds with no effect on grass.

• Have no soil-acting properties, and on contact with the soil they become harmless, enabling the soil to be re-cultivated shortly after application.

Disadvantages

• Short term rather than long term results.

• Have little or no effect on root systems. The roots of annual weeds are usually short and will thus wither with the plant. Perennial weeds appear dead when defoliated by this method but will subsequently re-shoot.

• Overall application to the entire plant is essential as they only kill on contact with live green tissue, e.g. if on a plant only one leaf is treated, that leaf alone will die.

• Have to be carefully applied to avoid contact with cherished plants.

• Application has to be repeated regularly to maintain continuous weed control.

Major brand names of products in this section:

Total contact weedkiller:
ICI Weedol (based on paraquat and diquat)

Selective contact weedkillers:
Murphy Mortegg—for moss and speedwell on turf (based on tar oil)

May & Baker Actrilawn—for annual weeds in newly sown turf (based on ioxynil)

Lawn Sand (various brands) (Based on ammonium sulphate and ferrous sulphate)

2. Translocated weedkillers

Translocated weedkillers are used to eradicate deeply-rooted weeds. Those used for lawn weed control such as 2,4-D, dichlorprop, MCPA and mecoprop are also known as hormone weedkillers, and work by stimulating and accelerating the growth rate of the weeds until they die. They are available in liquid form, as aerosols for spot weeding and in combination with lawn fertilizers. Another type of translocated weedkiller, aminotriazole, is found in some path weed control products, and this works by destroying the green chlorophyll in the plant. The effect on the plant is permanent, so perennials as well as annuals are killed completely. The newest forms of translocated weedkillers are those based on glyphosate. Glyphosate moves systemically throughout the entire plant system following application to the leaves, and is effective against grasses as well as broad-leaved weeds. Used selectively in the gel formulation, it can be applied as a spot treatment to individual weeds within a cherished plant environment. Glyphosate kills all weeds, including such persistent species as couch grass, ground-elder and horsetail, and works by preventing the manufacture of new plant food or the use of stored food reserves.

Advantages
• Totally eradicate the plant to which they are applied.
• Complete overall application to a plant is not essential for

control.

- Long term results, repeated applications rarely required.
- Individual spot treatment is possible.
- Glyphosate is inactivated on contact with soil. Re-cultivation is possible shortly after treatment.

Disadvantages

- It is a relatively slow method, taking up to 6 weeks with no immediate visible results.
- Have to be carefully applied to avoid contact with cherished plants.
- Need to be applied during dry period, without wind, to avoid drift.

Major brand names of products in this section:

Total translocated weedkillers:
Super Weedex (based on aminotriazole and simazine)
Tumbleweed (based on glyphosate)

Selective translocated weedkillers:
Murphy Lawn Weedkiller (based on 2,4-D and dichlorprop)
Tumbleweed Gel (based on glyphosate), n.b. selective by selective application.

3. Residual Weedkillers

These are applied directly to the soil, generally in advance of weed growth, to prevent weed development. Total residual weedkillers are used mainly for treating uncropped areas such as paths and drives where they remain active for up to 12 months. Selective residual weedkillers are applied to weed-free soil in specified cropping situations to prevent the growth of annual weeds from seed. Dichlobenil and simazine are used at full rate for total weed control, and at reduced rate for selective weed control in specified crops.

Advantages

- Very effective method of weed control.
- Long term results.

- Minimum number of applications necessary.

Disadvantages
- Ground treated by total, residual weedkillers cannot be used for any cultivation for 12 months.
- Have to be carefully applied to avoid harming the roots of cherished plants nearby.

Major brand names of products in this section:

Total residual weedkillers:
Synchemicals Casoron G (based on dichlobenil)
Weedex (based on simazine)
Sodium Chlorate
Selective residual weedkillers:
Murphy Covershield Weed Preventer (based on propachlor)
Casoron G and Weedex at selective rates in specified crop situations (see labels).

Trade mark acknowledgements:
Actrilawn is a trade mark of May & Baker Ltd.
Casoron is a registered trade mark of Philips-Duphar B.V., Amsterdam.
Weedol is a trade mark of Imperial Chemical Industries Ltd.

Covershield, Mortegg, Murphy, Super Weedex, Tumbleweed, Tumbleweed Gel and Weedex are trade marks.

Where to use these different chemical weedkillers

Now that we have discussed in detail the different types of chemicals available, how they work, and their advantages and disadvantages, let us take the different areas of the garden where you may have weed problems, and discuss which types should be used, and when they should be applied:

a. Cultivated ground i.e. Flower and vegetable areas

Type of weeds: Mainly annuals. Some perennials.

Treatment and Timing: Tumbleweed or Weedol for preparation before sowing and for careful inter-row, or surrounding area treatment—early spring or as necessary. Tumbleweed Gel for spot treatment—anytime. Covershield—after sowing or planting.

b. Herbaceous Borders

Type of weeds: Mainly perennials.

Treatment and Timing: Tumbleweed, applied with care to avoid contact with cultivated plants—when weeds large enough. Tumbleweed Gel for spot treatment—anytime.

c. Rose Beds

Type of weeds: Annuals and perennials.

Treatment and Timing: Tumbleweed or Weedol to clear early seedlings, followed by application of Covershield (or Weedex or Casoron G in rose-only beds)—spring.

d. Shrubberies

Type of weeds: Annuals and perennials.

Treatment and Timing: Tumbleweed or Weedol, carefully applied to weeds only—when weeds large enough. Tumbleweed Gel for spot treatment—anytime. Covershield to weed free soil—anytime. Weedex or Casoron G to certain shrubs if over 12 months established—spring, to weed-free soil.

e. Fruit Gardens (Orchards, fruit trees and bushes)

Type of weeds: Mainly perennials, especially perennial grasses.

Treatment and Timing: Weedex can be used around the bases of trees or bushes if established for 12 months—February and March. Tumbleweed with careful application for common couch, and other perennial weeds—May to October. Tumbleweed Gel for spot treatment—anytime.

f. Established Lawns

Type of weeds: Mainly perennials.

Treatment and Timing: Lawn Weedkiller—May to September as necessary. Tumbleweed Gel for spot treatment—anytime. Mortegg for speedwell control—May to September.

g. Newly Sown Lawns

Type of weeds: Annuals and perennials.

Treatment and Timing: Actrilawn for annual weeds. No treatment with any other weed-killer for first six months. Then Lawn Weedkiller on established lawns or Tumbleweed Gel for spot treatment.

h. Paths, Drives, Patios

Type of weeds: Annuals, perennials, persistent grasses.

Treatment and Timing: Tumbleweed, Super Weedex or Casoron G—spring. Tumbleweed Gel for spot treatment—anytime.

i. Neglected areas, waste ground

Type of weeds: All varieties.

Treatment and Timing: Tumbleweed, repeated if necessary—when weeds in growth. Or treat with Sodium Chlorate and leave for 12 months. Then apply Tumbleweed or Weedol prior to planting.

j. Brambles, elderberry, etc

Treatment: Tumbleweed towards end of season.

k. Problem Weeds

e.g. Common Couch, Colt's-foot, Creeping Thistle, Ground-elder, Horsetails.

Treatment: Tumbleweed as directed on label or repeated applications of Weedol. Spot treatment with Tumbleweed Gel.

The application of chemical weedkillers

There are several methods of applying chemical weedkillers. All are very straightforward, and the size and type of area dictates which type of applicator to use.

Watering cans

Watering cans provide the cheapest and most versatile method of application. By fitting a small variety of different roses, there are few situations requiring weed treatment (other than spot application) where a watering can cannot be used. For large areas such as neglected ground, lawns, drives or the preparation of cultivated vegetable or flower beds, use a watering can fitted with a wide dribble bar. For more discriminate application fit a short dribble bar or fine rose.

Mechanical dispensers

There are several different mechanical dispensers on the market. They have the advantage of applying weedkillers more uniformly as they remove some of the human element, but are, of course, fairly costly, at least in relation to the simple watering can. The following four types are the most common:

Roller applicator

Ideal for large lawns. A device which one pushes like a lawn mower, consisting of a large tank which dispenses weedkiller on to a wide roller and thus is subsequently transferred directly on to the ground, giving maximum contact coverage and no drift. Very efficient.

Granule distributor

Again for lawns, used for distributing lawn sand or weedkiller/fertilizer granules. A device which is pushed along and distributes the granules uniformly over the ground.

Half to two gallon pump-up sprayers

Consist of a plastic container and a pump to pressurise the diluted weedkiller. Has an adjustable nozzle to vary spray from coarse to fine. Ideal for general garden weedkilling, and can be fitted with a hood for more selective application.

Knapsack sprayers
Consist of a tank to contain up to four gallons of weedkiller solution. The tank is strapped to a person's back and has a long pipe and nozzle for hand operated, wide area application close to the ground. Ideal for treatment of very large areas.

Spray bottles
Ideal for situations where a small area needs careful application, but requires more than spot treatment. Will contain a limited amount of weedkiller solution and can be used on selective areas.

Spot treatment
This is useful where a translocated weedkiller needs to be applied to a specific plant or plants, so it is often painted directly on to the offending plant with a brush (e.g. paintbrush or built-in brush applicator). An alternative for spot treatment of lawn weeds is translocated weedkiller in a foaming aerosol.

The amount of weedkiller to use

All weedkiller products carry exact instructions on the measure to be used related to a specific area. For example it could be 2 fluid oz weedkiller, diluted in 2 gallons of water, will treat 20 square yards. Although it will take a little extra time, calculate the area you intend to treat and thus the amount of weedkiller you require. *Never* alter the manufacturer's recommendations concerning these dilution ratios.

General hints on application

Before applying a weedkiller it is worth measuring and marking out each area with lengths of string to ensure correct application. Remember, it is not always easy to see where you have been, so mark off as you spray to diminish the risk of double application to some areas and none to others.

The product label of any marketed weedkiller always carries

detailed instructions on its use, and these should be carefully observed. There are also some basic, commonsense rules which should be followed when using any garden chemical, and these briefly are:

1. Keep all herbicides out of reach of children and pets, ideally locked in a cupboard.

2. Do not store herbicides, particularly lawn weedkillers, in the greenhouse.

3. Always read the product label carefully before commencing use.

4. Do not handle herbicides in the kitchen, or fill sprayers or watering cans at the kitchen sink.

5. Return partly used containers of herbicides to safe storage —or certainly out of the reach of children—*before* you commence application.

6. Never transfer herbicides out of their original containers.

7. Do not apply herbicides in windy weather to avoid drift damage in your own, or neighbour's garden.

8. Do not spray herbicides on plants being visited by bees at flowering time.

9. Thoroughly wash out sprayers and watering cans used to apply herbicides with detergent and several rinses of clean water. It is very sensible to keep one watering can and sprayer solely for this purpose and clearly marked as such.

10. Dispose of all herbicide containers carefully. They should be washed out thoroughly once empty and placed directly into a refuse bin. Never re-use such a container for any other purpose.

11. Always wash hands thoroughly with soap and water after using any garden chemical.

n.b. : To obtain utmost efficiency from a foliage-applied chemical weedkiller, apply on a dry, settled day, when it is likely to remain dry for 6 hours after application.

Flower and vegetable areas

Most of the weeds found in these two specific areas are annuals. This is because we are dealing with cultivated areas which receive regular attention throughout the year, year in year out. Perennial weeds get less chance to propagate themselves when the soil has been well dug and tended and they have been disturbed. However, the fact that these areas are looked after also attracts the regular annual weeds who are delighted to find well fertilised, well kept soil—perfect for your prize chrysanthemums or Maris Pipers and ideal for intruders, too! Unfortunately, weeds tend to grow faster than most crops and plants so therefore not only do they compete for the essentials of healthy growth—food, air, water and space—but have more than a head start over their competition, *your* plants, smothering and de-vitalising them in their quest for success.

It is worth making one's basic preparation as thorough as possible. Start in early spring prior to any sowing when one has a clean bed of soil. Already it will contain a vast number of weeds just waiting for the ideal conditions of spring to start germinating. As soon as the ground is workable, fork through or rotavate, leaving the surface smooth. Leave for a few days and wait for the weed germination. Soon, tiny seed leaves will appear in profusion. Now is the time to treat the entire area with a short term non-selective contact or translocated weed-killer. This will completely kill all foliage with which it comes into contact, and their root systems, but will disintegrate when it touches the soil so will not harm it. A few days later fork over again and repeat once more. Then commence sowing. With vegetables there is a tendency to plant rows too close. Some experts advocate a minimum of one yard between each row, but few of us have this sort of area to be so generous! The tendency these days is to sow and plant much closer than a few years ago, but try to leave enough space to enable one to keep up the worthwhile inter-row weed treatment at regular intervals. A granular, selective, residual weedkiller (Cover-shield) can be applied to certain vegetable seed beds. Chemical weedkillers can continue to be used here if necessary through-out the growing season if carefully applied by watering can or spray. Remember, your crop cannot come to any harm if it does not come into direct contact with its foliage. Where Covershield is not recommended, the vegetable rows them-selves will, of course, have to be hand weeded or hoed. However, it is the between-row weeds which, if left un-checked, will grow profusely and cause the greatest threat to your cherished plants. Once your vegetable crop is well matured, overall weeding is not so important, but it is still worthwhile removing any flowering weed heads to prevent future seeding.

The same basic principles apply to your flower beds. Pre-paration is again an important factor, and early recognition of weed seedlings and their subsequent eradication will aid the growth of your flowers. If you are starting a completely fresh flower bed with no dormant perennials, early spring applica-tion of chemicals may be made and the ground treated in the same way as the vegetable areas. Once you have sown your flower seeds do not use a herbicide, but hand weed or hoe at as early a stage as possible. If, however, you are creating your flower areas with bedding plants, or have a variety of peren-nials emerging, Covershield can be used to deal with any propagating annuals, but it is better to kill perennial weeds selectively with a chemical gel rather than use an overall application.

The following weeds featured are among the most common to be found in these two areas. Throughout the book, each weed described is illustrated in colour at its mature stage, and details are given alongside which will (I hope!) help you to identify it with ease. In addition, I have included a line drawing and brief description of its seedling, where appropriate.

(It should be noted that the colour illustrations and seedling drawings are not in proportion in size, either to each other or to any other weeds or seedlings featured in the book.)

I have purposely avoided the use of too many technical words and classifications throughout the text and descriptions, to keep the book as simple and easy to read as possible. However, in some cases, and especially when describing the seedlings, there was no alternative but to use the technical name, but a full definition of all words used can be found at the back of the book.

Weeds featured in this section:

Annual Meadow-grass
Black-bindweed
Charlock
Cleavers
Common Chickweed
Common Fumitory
Common Poppy
Cow Parsley
Dandelion
Fat-hen
Field Bindweed
Germander Speedwell
Groundsel
Hairy Bitter-cress
Knotgrass
Nipplewort
Petty Spurge
Pineappleweed
Redshank
Scarlet Pimpernel
Scented Mayweed
Scentless Mayweed
Shepherd's-purse
Small Nettle
Smooth Sow-thistle
Spear Thistle

Annual Meadow-grass *Poa annua* Annual

Occurs as a basal clump of tightly-tufted, bright green, narrow, pointed leaves. The flower-heads have a fluffy appearance, are triangular in outline, and consist of many spikelets, each with numerous pale green or greenish-purple coloured seeds. Each flower-head grows at the top of a thin stem which rises above the clump of leaves. This grass also occurs commonly as a lawn weed.

n.b.: It has an extremely strong root and is almost impossible to weed by hand successfully.

Height at maturity
3″–12″ (8–30 cm).

Stem
Slender and weak.

Flowers
The flower-heads are triangular in outline and consist of many spikelets, each containing numerous greenish-purple or pale green seeds. Has an overall loose, feathery appearance. Flowers and seeds all the year round.

Leaves
Are long and narrow with sharp-pointed tips. There is a distinctive central fold to each leaf, and a ribbed appearance. Also, if held up to the light, one can see two parallel white lines, one each side of the centre fold.

Seedling
Occurs as a small single shoot, resembling the main plant in appearance.

Chemical Treatment
Kill with Tumbleweed or Tumbleweed Gel.
Prevent with Covershield.
Spot treat with Tumbleweed Gel when it appears as a lawn weed.

Annual Meadow-grass

Black-bindweed

Polygonum convolvulus   Annual

Other common name: Climbing buckwheat

Can occur as a climbing or prostrate spreading plant, which is composed of many long, sprawling stems growing from a single root. Each stem has numerous small, dark green, arrow-shaped leaves growing alternately along its length, with spiked clusters of greenish-red or greenish-white flowers occurring at the leaf axils.

Height at maturity
Length of stems: 24″–48″ (60–120 cm).

Stem
Slender, smooth and twining with a reddish tinge.

Flowers
Differ from Field and Hedge Bindweed in that they are not trumpet-shaped. (Incidentally, Black Bindweed is not botanically related to either of these weeds). They are small, greenish-red or greenish-white and occur in a loose spike of between 2 and 6 flower heads at each leaf axil. Flowers June to October.

Leaves
Are small, dark green and shaped like an arrow-head—pointed, triangular in outline and with pointed basal lobes. They grow on long stalks alternately along the length of the stem.

Seedling

Cotyledons long, narrow, and curve round in a crescent shape. True leaves arrow-shaped with rounded basal lobes. Hypocotyl crimson. The whole seedling is a reddish-green colour.

Chemical Treatment
Tumbleweed or Tumbleweed Gel.

26

Black-bindweed

Charlock   *Sinapis arvensis*   Annual

Other common names: Wild mustard, Karlock

An erect plant, distinguished by its stiff, hairy stem, large lower leaves which are hairy, stalked and coarsely toothed, and its bright yellow flowers which grow in clusters at the top of the stem and later develop into long, narrow seed pods.

Height at maturity
12″–36″ (30–90 cm).

Stem
Upright, branched and hairy.

Flowers
Bright sulphur yellow and occur in clusters at top of stems. They develop into long, narrow seed pods with slightly wavy edges, which split lengthways to emit shiny black seeds. Flowers May to August.

Leaves
The lower leaves are oval to lance-shaped, stalked, hairy and toothed. The upper leaves are stalkless and lance-shaped.

Seedling

Cotyledons heart-shaped and smooth. True leaves are hairy, have a broad rounded tip and shallow indentation to leaf edge.

Chemical Treatment
Tumbleweed or Tumbleweed Gel.

Charlock

Cleavers *Galium aparine* Annual

Other common names: Goosegrass, Sweethearts, Sticky Willie

A climbing, sticky plant, which has a square stem and whorls of between 6 and 8 narrow leaves along its length. It is best identified by its seed pods or burrs, which are small, round and green, covered with hooked hairs and thus attach themselves easily to clothing, animal fur, etc.

Height at maturity
8″–60″ (20–150 cm).

Stem
Climbing but rather weak and straggly. It is square, covered with hooked bristles and is a brownish-green colour tinged with red.

Flowers
Small white flowers occur in clusters from the leaf axils on the upper stem. These develop into round, green seed pods (which turn brownish when ripe) and are covered with hooked hairs. Flowers June to September.

Leaves
Are narrow, lance-shaped, and occur in whorls or rings of between 6 and 8 around the stem. They are also prickly along midrib and leaf edges.

Seedling

Cotyledons large, and round to oblong in shape. True leaves occur in a rose-shaped cluster, are oval to pointed, and hairy. The hypocotyl is very long.

Chemical Treatment
Kill with Tumbleweed or Tumbleweed Gel.
Prevent with Covershield.

Cleavers

Common Chickweed   *Stellaria media*   Annual

Other common name: Chickenweed

A straggling, prostrate, rather "matted" plant, with many weak stems. Each stem has a single line of hairs running down its length, and pairs of small, bright green, pointed, oval leaves along it. At the end of each stem grow small white flowers with 5 deeply divided petals which give the appearance of 10 individual ones. It seeds and reproduces abundantly and with its matted habit tends to smother other plants. It is also very difficult to pull out by hand without leaving the roots behind.

Height at maturity
Each flowering stem can grow to 12″ (30 cm) or more, but these usually lie flat on the ground.

Stems
Prostrate or semi-erect, very weak, and have a characteristic single line of hairs along them.

Flowers
Has small white flowers with 5 deeply divided petals and dark red stamens. This weed flowers all year round, but each individual flower only lasts about one day.

Leaves
Are pointed and oval in shape. Occur in pairs along stem, the lower leaves long-stalked, upper pairs stalkless.

Seedling

Cotyledons are smooth, oval and have a prominent mid-vein. True leaves more pointed and have long hairs on stalks. The whole seedling is a light bright green.

Chemical Treatment
Kill with Tumbleweed or Tumbleweed Gel.
Prevent with Covershield.

Common Chickweed

Common Fumitory *Fumaria officinalis* Annual

A delicate, feathery-looking, grey-green plant, which is basic-ally upright in habit, but can also spread. The leaves are linear, occurring in stalked leaflets which are multi-divided. Its small pink flowers are purple at the top and grow alternate-ly in spikes of approximately 20 flower heads.

Height at maturity
6″–15″ (15–40 cm).

Stem
Weak, smooth, slender and multi-branched with a spreading tendency. First tinged pink which changes to brown as the leaves develop.

Flowers
Has tiny pink flowers which are tinged purple at the top and grow alternately along stems in groups of about 20 flower heads to form a spray. Flowers June to September.

Leaves
Have the appearance of a feather, each "leaf" being multi-branched with ribbon-like leaflets. Silver grey/green in colour and waxy.

Seedling

Cotyledons are long and narrow. The true leaves are divided into segments. The whole seedling is a light blue-green.

Chemical Treatment
Tumbleweed or Tumbleweed Gel.

Common Fumitory

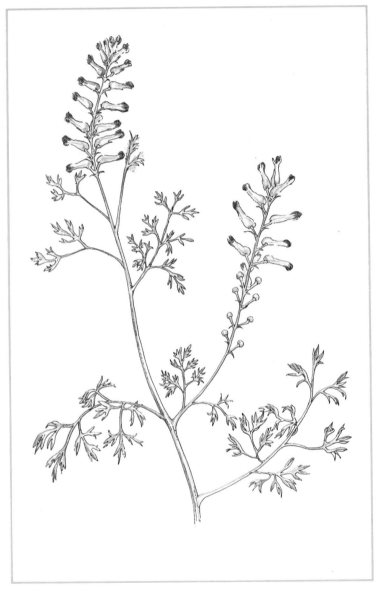

Common Poppy
Papaver rhoeas

Annual

Other common names: Field poppy, Corn rose

One of the most popular common weeds, easily recognised by its bright scarlet coloured flowers with black centres, tall, slender, bristly stems, and thin, ragged, hairy leaves. They usually grow in large groups and are a very striking sight when in bloom.

Height at maturity
12"–24" (30–60 cm).

Stem
Very long and slender. Branched, and covered with stiff, bristly hairs.

Flowers
Are very fragile, large, bright scarlet with a black centre, and grow on long stalks from leaf axils. The four petals sometimes have a black blotch on the inside. The flowers are followed by distinctive goblet-shaped seed heads. Flowers May to June.

Leaves
Grow alternately up stem, and are deeply cut into narrow segments giving a very ragged appearance. Covered with bristly hairs.

Seedling

Cotyledons smooth, narrow and linear. First sets of true leaves round to pointed, followed by hairy leaves with a single toothed indentation. Overall bluish-green in colour.

Chemical Treatment
Tumbleweed or Tumbleweed Gel.

Common Poppy

Cow Parsley

Anthriscus sylvestris   Biennial to Perennial

Other common names: Wild Parsley, Keck

An easily recognised weed by its size and dominance within its surroundings. Growing to an average height of about 30″ (75 cms), it has large, flat, umbrella-shaped clusters of tiny white flowers, a thick grooved stem, and large, soft, feathery-looking leaves which are composed of many leaflets. Its long tap roots make physical removal very difficult.

Height at maturity

24″–40″ (60–100 cm).

Stem

Stiff, erect, hollow, grooved and many-branched. The lower stem is downy, the upper stem smooth.

Flowers

Are tiny, white and occur in an umbrella shape which is composed of numerous clusters. Each cluster is carried on a long, thin stalk from a central axis at the end of a stem. Flowers April to June.

Leaves

Large, soft, bright green and often up to 12 inches (30 cm) long. Each leaf is divided into many leaflets which themselves are further divided into minute leaflets, thus giving a very feathery appearance. They alternate up the stem and emerge from sheaths.

Seedling

Cotyledons very long and narrow. First true leaves are divided into segments and are hairy.

Chemical Treatment
Tumbleweed or Tumbleweed Gel.

38

Cow Parsley

Dandelion *Taraxacum officinale* Perennial

One of our best-known weeds. Easily recognised by its rosette of lance-shaped, jagged-edged leaves, and large, yellow, multi-floreted flowers which turn into fluffy white balls at seeding stage. It has a strong, deep, tap root which will send up new leaves if broken. Also a very common lawn weed.

Height at maturity
6″–12″ (15–30 cm).

Stem
No true stem. The flower stalks are upright, round and smooth, and completely leafless. Contains a white, milky juice.

Flowers
Occur singly at the top of each stalk, are large, bright yellow, and composed of over a hundred florets. These turn into a seed head consisting of numerous seeds, each with fluffy hairs for easy dispersal. Flowers March to November.

Leaves
Lance-shaped and very deeply cut (or toothed). Smooth and stalkless, forming a rosette shape.

Seedling

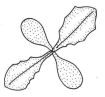 Cotyledons small and round. True leaves oval to pointed in shape, with slightly ragged edges. Overall dark green, shiny and completely hairless. Grows prostrate.

Chemical Treatment
Tumbleweed or Tumbleweed Gel.
Murphy Lawn Weedkiller or Tumbleweed Gel where it occurs as a lawn weed.

Dandelion

Fat-hen *Chenopodium album* Annual

Other common names: Lamb's quarters, Goosefoot

An erect, pyramid-shaped plant, silvery-green in colour, but with a dull "mealy" appearance to its leaves. Identifiable by its dense clusters of small green flowers which grow in sprays.

Height at maturity
Can vary greatly from about 6″ (15 cm) to 72″ (180 cm).

Stem
Erect, smooth and branched with a reddish tinge.

Flowers
Are tiny, round, green, and grow in dense clusters to form sprays. Flowers July to September.

Leaves
Vary considerably in shape. All tend to be silvery-green, dull and "mealy" in appearance, with a slightly reddish colouring underneath. Fleshy and short stalked, the lower leaves are wide, large and pointed. The upper leaves are long, narrow and pointed.

Seedling

Cotyledons long, narrow, and bright purple on the underside. First true leaves are spear-shaped, followed by a second pair which are more variable in shape, with slightly toothed edges. The hypocotyl is also a purple colour, and the whole seedling has a dull "mealy" appearance.

Chemical Treatment
Tumbleweed or Tumbleweed Gel.

Fat-hen

Field Bindweed   *Convolvulus arvensis*   Perennial

Other common name: Bellbine

A very common garden weed, easily recognised by its twining habit—it usually twists itself around another plant—vivid pink, or pink and white, trumpet-shaped flowers, and dark green, arrow-shaped leaves. Its deep, invasive roots are virtually impossible to dig out completely. Any broken fragments regrow.

n.b.: Is similar to Hedge Bindweed but much smaller and more compact.

Height at maturity
12″–24″ (30–60 cm).

Stem
Slender, smooth and twining. (n.b.: It always twists itself around another plant in an anti-clockwise direction).

Flowers
Grow on long stalks from the leaf axils, are trumpet-shaped, and bright pink, or pink and white, often with five purple stripes on the outside. Usually measuring about an inch (2.5 cm) long and in diameter, they are also slightly scented. Flowers June to September.

Leaves
Distinctly arrow-shaped with pointed basal lobes, approximately 1″–2″ long (2.5–5 cm) and dark green. Smooth, stalked and grow alternately along the stem.

Seedling

Cotyledons large and round with indented top. True leaves spade-shaped. Can also reproduce by shoots directly from root fragments.

Chemical Treatment
Tumbleweed or Tumbleweed Gel, repeating on new growth as necessary.

Field Bindweed

Germander Speedwell *Veronica chamaedrys* Perennial

Other common name: Bird's-eye

A plant which starts prostrate, roots at the nodes, and then sends up erect, slender stems which are particularly distinctive by the two lines of long, white hairs which occur on opposite sides. Has heart-shaped, hairy leaves occurring in pairs, and spikes of small, deep blue, white-centred flowers.

Height at maturity
3″–12″ (8–30 cm).

Stem
Prostrate, then semi-erect, rooting at nodes. Slender and have two lines of white hairs.

Flowers
Small, dark blue, usually with a white centre, and occur in spikes of between 10 and 20 individual flowers, each on its own short stalk. Flowers March to August.

Leaves
Dull green, heart-shaped and hairy, occurring in pairs up stem. Have soft-toothed edges.

Seedling

Cotyledons oval to pointed. True leaves occur in pairs, have softly-toothed edges, and are slightly hairy.

Chemical Treatment
Kill with Tumbleweed or Tumbleweed Gel.
Prevent with Covershield.

Germander Speedwell

Groundsel *Senecio vulgaris*   Annual

A ragged, rather untidy-looking plant, with its many-branched, upright stems, and ungainly, long, and coarsely-toothed stem leaves. The flowers are distinctive by their tubular shape and yellow heads, which develop into fluffy white seed heads.

Height at maturity
3″–15″ (8–38 cm).

Stem
Upright, smooth and succulent.

Flowers
Occur in close clusters of numerous tubular-shaped heads. They consist of thick tufts of yellow florets above a cylindrical-shaped green base. The flowers turn into fluffy white balls of seed heads. Flowers and seeds all year round.

Leaves
Stem leaves are long, ragged and coarsely-toothed. Smooth, or very slightly hairy, and stalkless.

Seedling

Cotyledons narrow, pointed and purple on underside. True leaves have step-like teeth and pointed top.

Chemical Treatment
Kill with Tumbleweed or Tumbleweed Gel.
Prevent with Covershield.

Groundsel

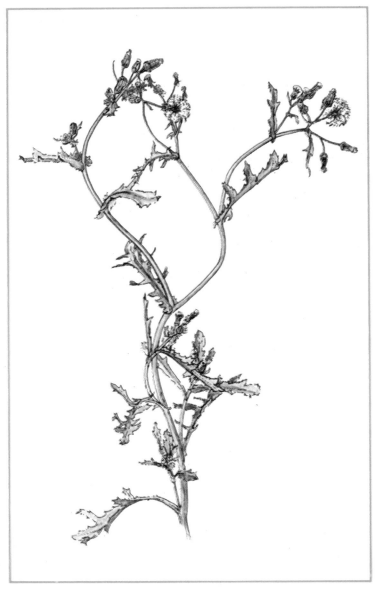

Hairy Bitter-cress *Cardamine hirsuta* Annual or Biennial

Other common name: Poppers

A hardy, small plant, which appears as a rosette of dark, round leaves in winter, but when flowering, produces a central, wavy stem topped by an insignificant white flower, which is over-shadowed by seed pods. It flowers and seeds when very small, thus producing more than one generation each year. The seed pods have a unique mechanism by which they explode and eject the seeds when ripe to a distance of up to 3 feet. It is a very common weed in compost of container-grown plants.

Height at maturity
6"–12" (15–30 cm).

Stem
The rosette is composed of numerous leaf-stalks, each bearing a number of leaflets. Single wavy, branched stems rise from the centre of the rosette of leaves.

Flowers
A small cluster of insignificant white flowers occurs at the top of the stem, but is overshadowed by numerous seed pods. Flowers April to September.

Leaves
Dark green, and almost round in shape, the leaflets have irregular indentations but no particular pattern. There are usually 7 leaflets on each stem, arranged in opposite pairs, with a single terminal leaflet which tends to be larger than the others. Massed together on individual stems, they form a flat rosette.

Seedling

Cotyledons round with indented top. True leaves kidney-shaped. Both cotyledons and true leaves have very long stalks.

Chemical Treatment
Tumbleweed or Tumbleweed Gel.

Hairy Bitter-cress

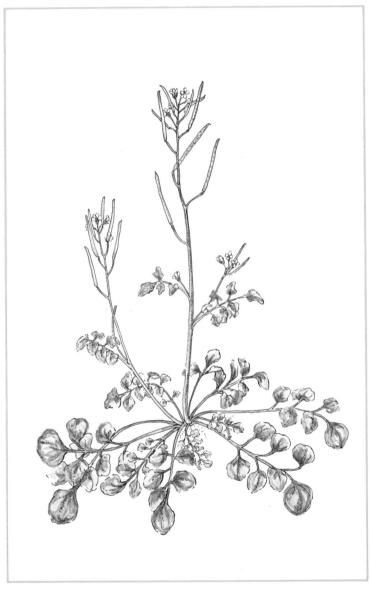

Knotgrass *Polygonum aviculare*   Annual

Other common names: Iron weed, Wire weed

A plant which adapts its style and appearance depending on its surroundings. On open ground with ample space it will grow prostrate and spreaded, while in fierce competition with other plants it will grow erect and tall. Identified by its tough stems which are swollen and reddish coloured at the joints, and also covered by silvery scales, its narrow, lance-shaped leaves, and tiny green flowers which occur in clusters of 2 to 5 in the leaf axils.

Height at maturity
2″–24″ (5–60 cm).

Stem
Many-branched and slender, but extremely tough. Tend to be swollen and reddish coloured at the nodes or leaf joints and have silvery scales.

Flowers
Grow in clusters of between 2 and 5 in the leaf axils, i.e. the point where the leaf stalk meets the stem. Are green, very tiny, and sometimes edged with pink or white. Flowers July to October.

Leaves
Dark green, narrow and lance-shaped, occurring alternately along the stem.

Seedling

Cotyledons long and narrow, with rounded ends. True leaves broad, spear-shaped and pointed. Hypocotyl long and crimson colour.

Chemical Treatment
Tumbleweed or Tumbleweed Gel.

Knotgrass

Nipplewort *Lapsana communis* Annual

A rather sparse-looking plant, consisting of slender, erect, and many-branched stems, single, large, ragged leaves which occur alternately, and branched clusters of small, pale yellow, dandelion-type flowers, each of which is supported by a long, thin stem.

Height at maturity
12″–36″ (30–90 cm).

Stem
Slender, erect and many-branched.

Flowers
Occur in branched clusters of up to 20 individual flower-heads, each supported by its own long, thin stem. Are pale yellow and rather flat—much smaller, but similar in appearance to the dandelion—and begin as tight, oval-shaped, green buds. The flowers open only under favourable conditions, i.e. light and warmth. Flowers May to September.

Leaves
The lower leaves are large, very ragged, slightly-toothed, and stalkless. The upper leaves are oval to lance-shaped, deeply-toothed and get progressively smaller up the stem. All the leaves alternate along the stem.

Seedling

Cotyledons small and oval, slightly indented at the top. True leaves are irregularly pointed and hairy. Soon forms a small rosette and the whole seedling is a yellowy colour.

Chemical Treatment
Tumbleweed or Tumbleweed Gel.

Petty Spurge   *Euphorbia peplus*   Annual

A delicate-looking, bright green plant, shaped rather like an open umbrella. Its upright stem is many-branched and further stalked with clusters of round-shaped leaves and tiny green flowers. Also at the point where each stem branches or re-branches grows a single pair of leaves.

n.b.: Similar and equally common is the **Sun Spurge** (*Euphorbia helioscopia*). This has a thicker but unbranched stem and generally grows taller.

Height at maturity
4″–12″ (10–30 cm).

Stem
Upright and many-branched—starting at any point from the root upwards. Contains a bitter, milky-white juice.

Flowers
No "flowers" in true sense. Minute, green, petal-less seed pods occur in the centre of each leaf cluster. "Flowers" May to October.

Leaves
Oval to round in shape and bright green, they grow in pairs to form clusters at end of stems. One solitary pair grows at each branching point of the stem, and single leaves grow alternately up the lower stems.

Seedling

Cotyledons oval-shaped with long stalks. True leaves round to pointed.

Chemical Treatment
Tumbleweed or Tumbleweed Gel.

Petty Spurge

Pineappleweed *Matricaria matricarioides* Annual

Other common names: Rayless mayweed, Rayless chamomile

Called the Pineappleweed due to its pungent smell, very like that of a pineapple, it is an erect plant with many feathery, "shredded ribbon" leaves, and button-like, yellowy-green flower-heads which have no petals or rays, (hence its other common names).

Height at maturity
2″–16″ (5–40 cm).

Stem
Erect, smooth and many-branched.

Flowers
Occur on short-stalked branches, usually in groups of three. Consist only of a flower-head of disk florets, greenish-yellow in colour, held on a hollow cone. No petals. Flowers May to November.

Leaves
Long and thin, cut into many ribbon-like segments. Grow densely up entire stem.

Seedling

Cotyledons small and oval. True leaves long, narrow, and with a single notch. Later pairs of leaves are more easily recognised, being more regularly lobed and shiny.

Chemical Treatment
Kill with Tumbleweed or Tumbleweed Gel.
Prevent with Covershield.

Pineappleweed

Redshank *Polygonum persicaria*   Annual
Other common names: Willow-weed, Persicaria

A rather attractive plant, with a definite reddish hue to its stem, and clusters of deep pink buds and flowers. Easily identified by its unique characteristic blotch on each leaf—which by legend represent drops of blood, as this plant was said to grow at the base of Christ's cross.

Height at maturity
10″–30″ (25–75 cm).

Stem
Upright, stiff and many-branched. Swollen at the nodes, from which grow both the leaves and flower stalks. The whole stem has a reddish colour.

Flowers
Deep pink and occur in clusters at top of stems. Flowers June to September.

Leaves
Long and narrow with distinctive blotch. Occur singly at each node.

Seedling

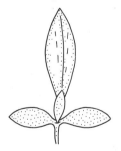

Cotyledons oval, pointed and held horizontally. It has a large, single, first true leaf, which is broad, oval to pointed, and sparsely hairy. The hypocotyl is bright scarlet.

Chemical Treatment
Tumbleweed or Tumbleweed Gel.

Redshank

Scarlet Pimpernel *Anagallis arvensis* Annual to Perennial

Other common name: Poor man's weather glass

A pretty plant which one may be tempted to leave rather than eradicate! Prostrate with many straggling stems, it has small, dark green, glossy leaves and tiny, bright red or pink flowers.

Height at maturity
3"–12" (5–30 cm).

Stem
Prostrate or semi-erect, branched and smooth.

Flowers
Small, bright red or pink (although occasionally blue), they occur singly on slender stalks all along the stems. Flowers May to October.

Leaves
Grow in pairs, are oval, pointed and a dark, glossy green. Smooth and stalkless, the underside of each leaf is dotted with black glands.

Seedling

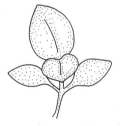

Cotyledons pointed oval shape. True leaves are triangular to heart-shaped and have black spots on underside. The whole seedling is a shiny dark green.

Chemical Treatment
Kill with Tumbleweed or Tumbleweed Gel.
Prevent with Covershield.

Scarlet Pimpernel

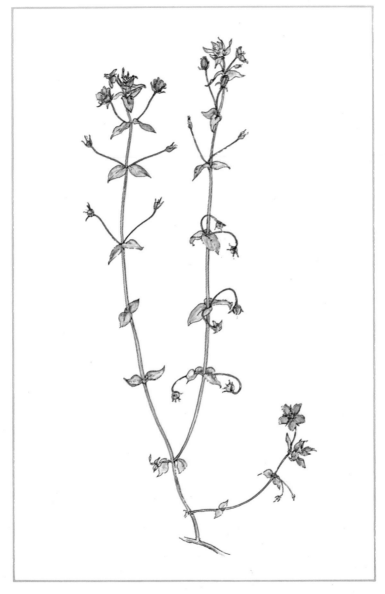

Scented Mayweed   *Matricaria recutita*   Annual

Other common name: Wild chamomile

An erect plant, which has several stiff stems growing directly from the root base. The stem is many-branched and single daisy-like flowers grow in groups, but each on a solitary stem. The leaves are feathery and divided into many thread-like segments. It has a sweet smell.

Height at maturity
6″–24″ (15–60 cm).

Stems
Stiff, erect and branched. Several stems grow from root base.

Flowers
Daisy-like, with white petals and yellow centre. The petals tend to droop downwards very quickly. Although the flowers occur in groups, each one is on a solitary stalk, and the flower-head is approximately $\frac{3}{4}$″ (2 cm) in diameter. Flowers May to October.

Leaves
Very fine and feathery in appearance, being divided into many ribbon-like segments.

Seedling

Cotyledons small and oval. First leaves long with oval tip and sparsely-lobed. Second pair of leaves multi-lobed.

Chemical Treatment
Kill with Tumbleweed or Tumbelweed Gel.
Prevent with Covershield.

Scented Mayweed

Scentless Mayweed

Annual to Perennial

Tripleurospermum maritimum subsp. inodorum
Other common name: Dog daisy

An erect, many-branched plant with flat, daisy-like flowers, each on a solitary stem. The leaves are very fine and feathery. Unlike the other members of its family, it has no scent.

Height at maturity
4"–24" (10–60 cm).

Stem
Erect, smooth, ribbed and many-branched.

Flowers
Flat and daisy-like in appearance, with white petals and a bright yellow centre, they usually measure about 1" (2·5 cm) in diameter. Flowers June to October.

Leaves
Are long and divided into many fine, feathery segments.

Seedling

Cotyledons flat oval shape. True leaves lobed.

Chemical Treatment
Kill with Tumbleweed or Tumbleweed Gel.
Prevent with Covershield.

Scentless Mayweed

Shepherd's-purse *Capsella bursa-pastoris*

Annual
to Biennial

This plant has a distinctive appearance with its flat rosette of deeply-toothed basal leaves, and prominent, upright stems which have heart-shaped seed pods growing directly from them up the entire length. The top of the stem is crowned with a cluster of tiny white flowers.

Height at maturity
3"–18" (8–45 cm).

Stem
Stems are upright, branched and slightly hairy.

Flowers
Clusters of tiny white flowers occur at the top of stems, followed by distinctive heart-shaped seed pods. Can flower all year round, but mainly from February to November.

Leaves
Are dark green, lance-shaped, and clasp stem. At young stage the leaves are slightly toothed, deepening as the plant matures. The basal leaves are narrow, deeply-toothed and form a flat rosette.

Seedling

Cotyledons rounded oval shape. True leaves almost round. Later leaves have irregularly-toothed margins. The whole seedling is a silvery-grey colour, often tinged with purple, and occurs as a semi-prostrate rosette.

Chemical Treatment
Kill with Tumbleweed or Tumbleweed Gel.
Prevent with Covershield.

Shepherd's-purse

Small Nettle *Urtica urens*

Annual

Other common name: Annual nettle

An unsociable plant due to its ability to sting and hurt. Easily identified by its leaves, which have regular, deep-toothed edges at a very early stage, and stinging hairs. Clusters of small green flowers occur at the leaf axils. Hand weeding is not recommended without wearing gloves!

Height at maturity
6"–24" (15–60 cm).

Stem
Upright, branched and covered with stinging hairs.

Flowers
Small green flowers occur in clusters of individual spikes at the leaf axils along the stems. Flowers June to September.

Leaves
Are oval, coarsely-toothed, stalked and covered with stinging hairs. Close observation of the leaf can identify this nettle from the Common Nettle (Perennial or Stinging Nettle) as all the veins run in direct lines to the tip. On the leaf of the Common Nettle the veins are branched.

Seedling

Cotyledons round to pear-shaped. True leaves have clearly-pointed teeth and long hairs.

Chemical Treatment
Kill with Tumbleweed or Tumbleweed Gel.
Prevent with Covershield.

Small Nettle

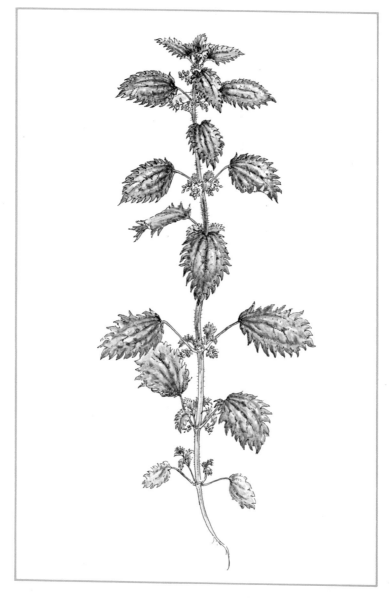

Smooth Sow-thistle *Sonchus oleraceus* Annual

Other common name: Milk thistle

A tall, rather chunky plant, with a thick but hollow stem containing a milky juice, large, ragged, prickly leaves and clusters of pale yellow flower heads which develop into downy seedheads with brownish-white hairs.

Height at maturity
24″–36″ (60–90 cm).

Stem
Thick, erect and hollow except at joints. Is branched, has a somewhat ribbed appearance and contains a milky juice.

Flowers
Grow in clusters at top of stems, and are encased in a distinctive green cone of sepals (technical name—involucre), emerging as a flat, pale yellow flower similar to a dandelion in appearance. In flower June to September, it is interesting to note that the flowers themselves are open only from 6 to 11 o'clock each morning.

Leaves
Large and very ragged in appearance. The main leaves are distinctly lobed, resulting in an almost arrow-shaped head, have a prominent mid-rib and razor-toothed, prickly edges. Stalkless. The upper leaves clasp the stem and are unlobed, but retain the prickly-toothed edge.

Seedling

Cotyledons round to oval-shaped. True leaves have very long stalks, are overall round in shape with lightly-toothed edges, and slightly hairy.

Chemical Treatment
Kill with Tumbleweed or Tumbleweed Gel.
Prevent with Covershield.

Smooth Sow-thistle

Spear Thistle *Cirsium vulgare* Biennial

Other common name: Scotch thistle

Large, erect, extremely prickly and fierce-looking plant. It
has coarse, ragged, pointed leaves with long, sharp spikes at
the tip, a thick, prickly stem and large, deep purple flowers
encased in a spiny, oval base shaped rather like a vase. At
young (first year) stage it appears as a flat rosette of coarse,
prickly leaves.

Height at maturity
24″–48″ (60–120 cm).

Stem
Upright, thick, grooved and prickly.

Flowers
Large flower-heads occur singly or in clusters of 2 or 3. The
top of flower is soft and a deep purple-red colour. The large,
green, oval base (involucre) is hard and covered with spines.
The flowers wither to produce downy off-white seedheads.
At the base of the involucre on each flower are two spear-like,
pointed leaves. Flowers July to August.

Leaves
Are lance-shaped and deeply, raggedly cut into narrow lobes,
each of which ends in a sharp spike. They alternate up the
stem.

Seedling

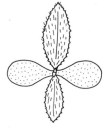

Cotyledons oval-shaped. The second true
leaf is much larger than its partner and is a
dull dark green with dense whitish hairs
on upper surface. The whole seedling
is prostrate.

Chemical Treatment
Tumbleweed or Tumbleweed Gel.

Spear Thistle

Herbaceous borders, rose beds, trees and shrub areas present a different type of weed problem. Of course, they too attract annual weeds, and any of the weeds mentioned in the previous section are likely to be found here also. However, unlike cultivated areas, where the gardener's attention is focused on the soil, here his work is centred above ground level in tending established plants. He has little reason to disturb the soil on any regular basis. Thus, like their bedmates, the main weeds that are found in these areas are also of the perennial variety, i.e. those whose roots creep deep into the soil, establishing themselves, and regrowing in spring or summer each year. And what could be more perfect? No disturbance, and the kindly gardener regularly feeding the surrounding soil with all sorts of goodness in the form of assorted fertilizers.

Hence your problem here is literally deep rooted. Once you have identified the weeds you are dealing with, it is worth tackling them thoroughly. It is important to eradicate as much established root as possible without causing any harm to your cherished plants. Here more laboured application is called for, and this is the ideal situation for the chemical weedkiller which comes in a gel form which you paint directly on to individual weeds. True, this takes time, but with well-established perennials it is not wasted effort, as by the method previously explained it will kill the entire plant it is applied to, right through its root system. I've found it is surprising how many weeds one can in fact deal with at one session, and I also discovered that it is quite an enjoyable artform! If, however, a touch of the Van Goghs does not appeal, similar results can, of course, be achieved by very careful application of herbicides by a watering can or spray. The benefits your plants will gain are immense with the removal of such vigorous competition for vital root space and nutrients.

Weeds featured in this section:

Broad-leaved Dock
Colt's-foot
Common Couch
Common Nettle
Common Ragwort
Creeping Thistle
Field Horsetail
Ground-elder
Hedge Bindweed
Japanese Knotweed
Lesser Celandine
Oxalis
Red Dead-nettle
Rosebay Willowherb
White Dead-nettle

Broad-leaved Dock   *Rumex obtusifolius*   Perennial

Other common name: Common dock

A tough-looking, erect plant with a stiff stem and numerous wide spreading branches. The leaves are large, oval-shaped, have slightly wavy edges, and reduce in size up the plant, giving it a pyramid outline. It also has very conspicuous thick clusters of brownish-green flowers growing at regular intervals up the plant. It has a strong, deep tap root which will regrow if broken, or incompletely removed.

Height at maturity
24″–36″ (60–90 cm).

Stem
Erect, very tough, ribbed and branched.

Flowers
Has dense clusters of tiny brownish-green flowers which turn into seed pods. Each cluster is subtended by a leaf.

Leaves
The base leaves are large, stalked, broadly oval-shaped and hairy, reducing in size and also becoming narrower as they grow up the stem.

Seedling

Cotyledons long and narrow. True leaves spade-shaped with long stems. The whole seedling is large, and often tinged deep crimson.

Chemical Treatment
Tumbleweed or Tumbleweed Gel just before flowering.

Colt's-foot *Tussilago farfara* Perennial

A common weed, but with unusual characteristics, the main one being that it produces flowers before leaves. These appear at the top of thick, scaly stems which shoot directly from the root base during February and March. They are bright yellow and resemble a cross between a daisy and a dandelion, subsequently withering into round, fluffy seed heads. Large, long-stemmed, heart-shaped, ragged-edged leaves follow, and these too are unusual as the underside of the leaf is covered with a type of white felt not unlike cotton wool. It has deeply seated roots and spreading underground shoots (stolons).

Height at maturity 6″ (15 cm) at flowering stage, to 14″ (35 cm) at fruiting.

Stem The flowering stems are stiff, erect, and covered with alternate pinky scales, which may be also covered with loose white cotton. These stems grow taller at fruiting. The true stem runs underground.

Flowers Occur singly at the top of each flowering stem, are bright yellow, many-floreted and approximately 1 inch (2·5 cm) in diameter. After flowering the heads droop, but become erect again at fruiting. Flowers February to March.

Leaves Are large, 4–10 inches (10–20 cm) across, very long-stalked and again grow directly from root base. Heart-shaped, they have an irregular, jagged edge, clear veining, and a loose, white, cotton substance underneath.

Seedling

Cotyledons oval and stalked. The true leaves are a pointed spade-shape, with slightly lobed edges, and covered with a white fluff. One true leaf is much larger than the other.

Chemical Treatment
Tumbleweed or Tumbleweed Gel when in full leaf.

Colt's-foot

Common Couch *Agropyron repens* Perennial

Other common names: Couch grass, Twitch, Scutch, Wicks and many other local variations

One of the gardener's worst enemies! A vigorous, spiky grass which grows from a tuft. Recognisable by its stiff, erect, slender stems, long, thin, rough leaves and spikes of green flowers. It has fleshy, white, underground stems which creep and re-root profusely.

Height at maturity
12″–30″ (30–75 cm).

Stem
Stiff, erect, slender and smooth.

Flowers
Occur in spikes at top of stems. The "spikelets" are green and are arranged alternately on opposite sides of the stem. Flowers July to September.

Leaves
Long, thin, dull green and blade-like, with a deep central crease, they grow alternately up the stem. They also have an unpleasant, rough feel to the touch.

Seedling
Occurs as single shoot, resembling the main plant (without flower spikes) in appearance.

Chemical Treatment
Tumbleweed or Tumbleweed Gel when at least 4–6 inches (10–15 cm) of active growth. In established shrubberies prevent with Casoron G.

Common Couch

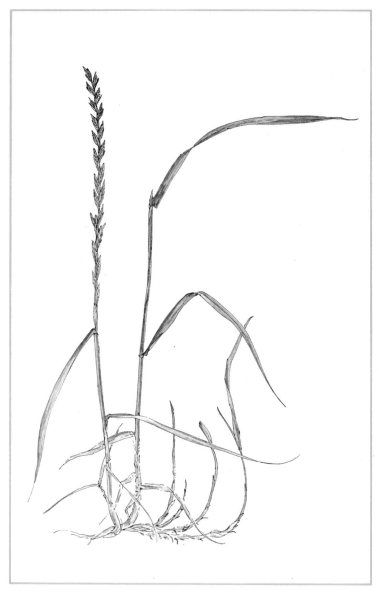

Common Nettle *Urtica dioica* Perennial

Other common name: Stinging nettle

A larger, more dominant and ugly plant than the Small Nettle, but again has the ability to sting. The leaves are broadly lance-shaped, deeply-toothed and covered with stinging hairs. Dull green, they have a downy appearance. Tassles of minute green flowers occur at the leaf axils. It can appear dead when defoliated but reshoots.

Height at maturity
24″–48″ (60–120 cm).

Stem
Stiff, upright and covered with bristly stinging hairs.

Flowers
Occur in hanging sprays of tiny green flowers at the leaf axils. Flowers June to September.

Leaves
Occur in pairs along stem and are broadly lance-shaped with coarsely-toothed edges. Are stalked, covered in stinging hairs and have a dull, downy appearance. All the veins on the leaf are branched, unlike the Small Nettle where the veins run in a direct line to the tip.

Seedling

Cotyledons small and round with indented top. True leaves are hairy, with rounded lobes and apex. Second pair of true leaves have pointed lobes more like the Small Nettle.

Chemical Treatment
Tumbleweed or Tumbleweed Gel when new growth is about 9 inches (22 cm) high. Later in season, cut down to soil level and treat the re-growth. In established shrubberies prevent with Casoron G.

Common Nettle

Common Ragwort
Senecio jacobaea Perennial

Other common names: Rag weed, Stinking Billie

A tall, overall ragged plant, which has a basal rosette of deeply cut, toothed leaves, and an erect, tough stem which culminates in clusters of numerous, yellow, daisy-like flowers. It is poisonous to livestock.

Height at maturity
8″–48″ (20–120 cm).

Stem
Erect, tough and branched at top.

Flowers
Occur in clusters at top of stems, are bright yellow, daisy-like and numerous. Flowers July to October.

Leaves
Overall lance-shaped, but deeply and irregularly cut, and coarsely toothed. Basal leaves are stalked and form a rosette. Stem leaves are similar in appearance but smaller and stalkless.

Seedling

Cotyledons round to oval in shape and slightly indented at top. True leaves are oval, have slightly wavy edges and are short stalked.

Chemical Treatment
Tumbleweed or Tumbleweed Gel.
Murphy Lawn Weedkiller where it appears in grass areas.

Common Ragwort

Creeping Thistle *Cirsium arvense* Perennial

A tall, erect plant—averaging 24″ (60 cm) high—with a fleshy, spiky stem, topped by clusters of pale purple flowers which later mature into downy, white seed heads, and lance-shaped, very prickly leaves. Similar to the Spear Thistle in appearance but less "heavy"-looking. A troublesome weed, very difficult to eradicate due to its ability to re-shoot from the smallest fragment of broken root. It has a slender tap root initially, which is followed by far-spreading underground horizontal roots lying about 12″ (30 cm) below the soil surface. These send up numerous shoots along their lengths.

Height at maturity
12″–48″ (30–120 cm) but averaging 24″ (60 cm).

Stem Upright, fleshy and covered with spikes.

Flowers
Occur in clusters of 2 to 4 on short stalks at top of stems. A dull, pale purple, they tend to spread into a flat tuft above the involucre, which is composed of many overlapping purple-green bracts. On maturity, they turn into downy, white seed heads although most of the seeds are sterile. The flowers have a strong, sweet smell. Flowers July to October.

Leaves
Basal leaves are large, lance-shaped, and very ragged, borne on short stalks. Upper leaves are similar, but smaller and clasp stem. All are very prickly and have a dominant central spine.

Seedling

Cotyledons large and oval, with marked mid-rib. True leaves oval, lobed, and have sharp spikes on the edges. It spreads by far-creeping roots which can readily regenerate new plants from small pieces, rarely by seed (which are usually sterile.)

Chemical Treatment
Tumbleweed or Tumbleweed Gel when in active growth.
In established shrubberies prevent with Casoron G.

Creeping Thistle

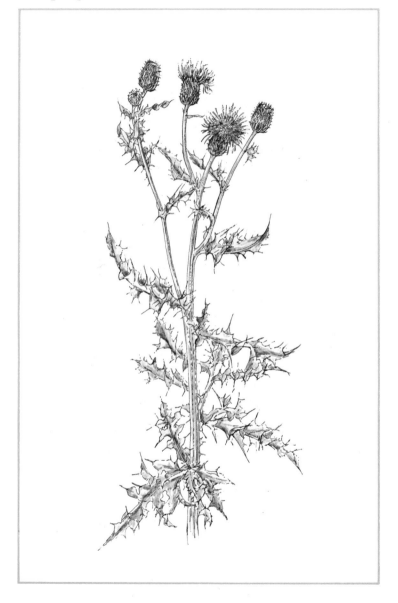

Field Horsetail *Equisetum arvense* Perennial

Other common names: Mare's-tail, Cat's or Rat's-tail

One of the stranger-looking plants, with no leaves or flowers in the true sense. Consists of a stiff, central, hollow stem which bears whorls of smaller bristly branches. These whorls decrease in size up the length of the stem, giving it an overall triangular outline. Has vigorous underground runners and spreads rapidly.

Height at maturity
12"–24" (30–60 cm).

Stem
The plant produces two different types of stem. The fertile stems develop in spring and early summer, have no branches, and reach 4–10 inches (10–25 cm), topped by a yellow-brown cone containing spores. Once the spores are dispersed, these stems wither, and sterile stems grow to 12–24 inches (30–60 cm). The central stem is stiff, erect and hollow except at the joints. It bears whorls of branches, each with the same jointed appearance as the main stem.

Flowers
No true flowers, but a yellow cone which turns brown at maturity, 1–4 cm long.

Leaves
None. Branches are tubular and jointed.

Seedling
None as such. Vegetative reproduction, or development from spores.

Chemical Treatment
Tumbleweed or Tumbleweed Gel from end of June.
On paths and uncropped areas use Super Weedex.
In established shrubberies prevent with Casoron G.

Field Horsetail

Ground-elder
Aegopodium podagraria   Perennial

Other common names: Goutweed, Bishop's weed

One of the gardener's worst enemies, as it is so common and persistent in its growth. Recognisable by its erect, grooved, hollow stems, and bright green, saw-edged leaves which usually occur in groups of three. During its flowering period it has clusters of tiny, white, star-shaped flowers which form an umbrella shape.

Height at maturity 16″–40″ (40–100 cm).

Stem
Erect, hollow and grooved (rather like a thin celery stalk). n.b.: Underground rooting stems are particularly vigorous and can cover several square yards from each plant.

Flowers
Grow in clusters and are tiny, white, and star-shaped. 15 or more clusters grow from the same axis, forming an umbrella shape. The flowers mature into tiny seed heads. Flowers May–July.

Leaves
Oval, pointed, and saw-edged. Bright green and tend to grow in groups of three. Stalked.

Seedling

Cotyledons long and narrow. True leaves are long-stalked and composed of three "leaflets", each one lobed. Again one true leaf is larger than its pair.

Chemical Treatment
Tumbleweed or Tumbleweed Gel when leaves have unfolded in late spring. Later in season, cut down to soil level and treat regrowth.
In established shrubberies prevent with Casoron G.

Ground-elder

Hedge Bindweed *Calystegia sepium* Perennial

Other common names: Convolvulus, Bellbine

A vigorous climbing and twisting plant—pretty to look at with its large, white, trumpet-shaped flowers, and deep green, pointed, heart-shaped leaves. Unfortunately its beauty belies its nature which is to strangle and smother all other plants in its quest for success. It also has deep, invasive roots which are virtually impossible to dig out completely. Any broken fragments will regrow.

Height at maturity
Almost immeasurable. Will continue to grow depending on its circumstances and environment. Has been recorded to reach the top of a tree!

Stem
Thin, twisting and twining in an anti-clockwise spiral manner, usually around another plant or up fencing.

Flowers
Large, white and trumpet-shaped, approximately 2″ (5 cm) in diameter. Flowers June–August.

Leaves
Are large, dark green, heart-shaped and pointed, growing alternately along the stem. They turn a golden yellow colour in autumn.

Seedling

Cotyledons long stalked, spade-shaped, but with a flat top. The true leaves are a pointed spade-shape and occur alternately up the shooting stem.

Chemical Treatment
Tumbleweed or Tumbleweed Gel when in full, active growth.
In established shrubberies, prevent with Casoron G.

Hedge Bindweed

Japanese Knotweed *Polygonum cuspidatum* Perennial
Other common name: Japanese bamboo

Possibly the least-common weed in this book, and will not be found in every garden. However, it has been included because where it does occur, it is a very troublesome and overpowering weed which needs checking or it can be difficult to eradicate. If it does grow in your garden you will not miss it, as it spreads rapidly underground and quickly forms large colonies, growing up to 9 feet high (270 cm). It has large, heart-shaped, pointed leaves, and when flowering, dense clusters of creamy-white, feathery-looking flowers.

Height at maturity
6–9 feet (180–270 cm)

Stem
Bamboo-like, stiff, erect and hollow, they are green with purple/red markings, but turn a striking brownish-red in winter.

Flowers
Are tiny, creamy-white, and occur in dense, branched, feathery-looking clusters approximately 5″ (12 cm) long, which grow directly from the nodes. Flowers July to October.

Leaves
Are very large and can be up to 12″ (30 cm) long. Overall heart-shaped, pointed and stalked, they grow alternately up the stems.

Seedling
This plant has an unusual reproduction system in that it produces seeds and subsequent seedlings, but mainly reproduces vegetatively, as the seedlings tend to perish after germination.

Chemical Treatment
Tumbleweed or Tumbleweed Gel when in maximum growth.

Japanese Knotweed

Lesser Celandine *Ranunculus ficaria* Perennial

Occurs in dense clusters of glossy, dark green, heart-shaped leaves and bright yellow, star-shaped flowers. Both leaves and flowers are individually stalked directly from the root. A pretty, but troublesome plant due to its ability to re-root and spread rapidly, giving a mat-like covering. It produces numerous bulbils which are easily spread by digging.

Height at maturity
2"–6" (5–15 cm).

Stem
Smooth and slender.

Flowers
Star-shaped and bright glossy yellow. Occur singly on thin stalks among clumps of leaves. Flowers February to April. The first flowers appear before the leaves.

Leaves
Heart-shaped, with slightly wavy edges, dark green and highly glossy. Occur in dense clumps, but each one is individual, growing on a thin stalk from the root.

Seedling

Cotyledons small and oval. True leaves spade-shaped but with a wavy edge. In a garden environment it usually reproduces from the bulbils, and not seeds.

Chemical Treatment
Tumbleweed or Tumbleweed Gel when in full leaf.

Lesser Celandine

Oxalis   *Oxalis corymbosa*   Perennial

Resembles a clover in appearance. The whole plant grows from a single "parent" bulb resembling a white carrot, from which numerous, tiny, stalkless bulbils develop attached to its crown. When detached by hoeing, digging, etc, each bulbil produces a large, trifoliate, hairy leaf, which can further be identified by looking on its underside where one will see tiny pink spots all around the edge. Purple-pink flowers occur in short clusters on long stalks, again from the parent bulb. Due to the spread of bulbils it is virtually impossible to eradicate this weed by mechanical means.

Height at maturity
6″–12″ (15–30 cm).

Stem
Tall, fluffy and covered with hairs.

Flowers
Are purple-pink in colour, and occur in a small cluster from a central axis at the top of a long stem direct from the parent bulb. Each flower, which is trumpet-shaped, is supported by a long, thin stalk to the axis. Flowers July to September.

Leaves
Are large and trifoliate, i.e. have three leaflets. Each leaflet is heart-shaped and hairy, and can measure 1″–2″ (2·5–5 cm) wide. On the underside of the leaf are tiny pink or red spots all round the edge.

Seedling
None as such. Reproduces directly from the bulb, which is composed of many tiny bulbils and has a white, carrot-like root.

Chemical Treatment
Tumbleweed of Tumbleweed Gel when in full leaf. Leafless bulbils may not be fully controlled, so repeat treatment when they produce leaves.

Oxalis

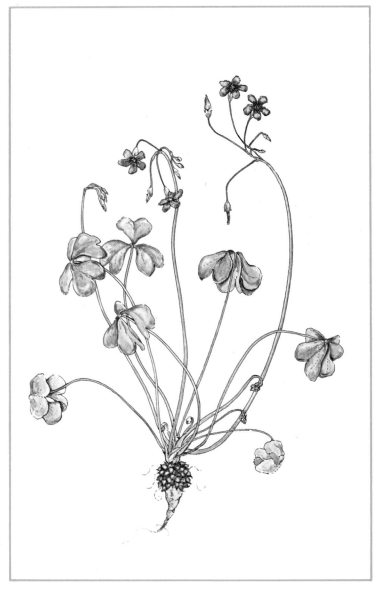

Red Dead-nettle *Lamium purpureum* Annual

An erect, spreading plant, with many stems branching out directly from the root base. Identified by its square, purplish-tinged stems, and pyramid-shape clusters of small, bright pink or red flowers intermingled with a mass of purple-tinged, heart-shaped leaves, which occur at the top of each stem. Larger heart-shaped leaves grow at intervals down the stem. All the leaves are softly hairy but do not sting. Has quite a strong smell.

Height at maturity
4″–18″ (10–45 cm).

Stem
Erect, square, purple-tinged, branched, and grows directly from the root base.

Flowers
Small, bright pink or red, occur among leaf clusters at top of each stem. Flowers April to October, but can continue into winter.

Leaves
Heart-shaped, pointed and round-toothed. At the top of the stem they are very small, purple-tinged and grow in great profusion. They increase in size and decrease in number down the length of the stem. All are wrinkled-looking and softly hairy.

Seedling

Cotyledons long-stalked and round, with a tiny point at apex and pointed basal lobes. True leaves also long-stalked, slightly toothed and have branched veins.

Chemical Treatment
Kill with Tumbleweed or Tumbleweed Gel.
Prevent with Covershield.

102

Red Dead-nettle

Rosebay Willowherb *Epilobium angustifolium* Perennial
Other common name: Fireweed

A tall, rather beautiful-looking plant, with its erect, pinkish stem and spire of vivid, pinky-mauve flowers. It spreads widely by long horizontal roots and grows to an average of 48″ tall, beginning with a spiral of long, lance-shaped leaves. The flowers start blooming about mid-way up the stem, mature and die away into long, tubular, pink-tinged seed pods, which open to release numerous wind-borne, white, plumed seeds. The plant continues flowering and seeding in this manner until the top is reached.

n.b.: This weed often occurs in areas where there has been a fire, hence its other common name "Fireweed".

Height at maturity
48″ (120 cm) or more.

Stem
Stiff, erect, unbranched and a pinky-red colour.

Flowers
Bright vivid pink, and grow on short stalks from the middle of the stem to the top. They commence flowering mid-way and work their way up, maturing into long, tubular seed pods as they go. Flowers June to September.

Leaves
Long, narrow and lance-shaped, they grow in a spiral around the stem base to about half way up the stem.

Seedling

Cotyledons pear-shaped and pointed. True leaves large, usually with two pairs of slight marginal teeth.

Chemical Treatment
Tumbleweed or Tumbleweed Gel.

Rosebay Willowherb

White Dead-nettle   *Lamium album*   Perennial

An erect, square-stemmed, softly hairy plant, with alternate pairs of large, pointed, coarsely-toothed, heart-shaped leaves. Each pair of leaves sits at right angles to the pair above and below. Clusters of white flowers occur in whorls around the stem at the leaf axils. This plant does not sting. It spreads vigorously by creeping underground stems (rhizomes).

Height at maturity
8″–24″ (20–60 cm).

Stem
Square, erect, hairy and unbranched.

Flowers
Occur in clusters of 6–8 in whorls around stem at leaf axils. Overall tubular in shape, they open at the top like a mouth. The upper lip forms a hood, the lower lip resembles a tongue and is divided into two lobes. Flowers March to November.

Leaves
Large, pointed, heart-shaped and coarsely-toothed. Always occur in pairs, each pair being set at direct right angles to the pair above. Decrease in size towards top of the plant.

Seedling

Cotyledons long-stalked, oval, and have distinctive pointed basal lobes. True leaves also long-stalked, hairy and round-toothed.

Chemical Treatment
Tumbleweed or Tumbleweed Gel.

White Dead-nettle

Section 3-Weeds in lawns

Weeds in lawns probably present the most annoyance to the average gardener. Lawns provoke a love/hate sort of relationship anyway—few would deny that a great deal of personal satisfaction is achieved when one stands back to admire one's newly mown lawn, with the smell of the fresh grass cuttings still in one's nostrils. Likewise, most of us experience a feeling of exasperation and despair when we observe the same lawn on the next day covered with daisies, clover and dandelions in profusion, to say nothing of numerous other prolific weeds less immediately obvious to the eye with their like green colouring, but equally industrious! The types generally found here tend to be very resilient and hardy and have the ability to adapt themselves easily to any conditions. For example, plantains, daisies and dandelions on lawns tend to grow flat on the ground—and in many cases escape the mower. Also the creeping type of weed, such as speedwell, mouse-ear chickweed and pearlwort actually root at each leaf joint to secure themselves safely into a lawn. As has been stated earlier, weeds are strong and usually find grass no competition to their easy development, and thus the grass tends to be stifled by their vigorous growth and obviously suffers.

Lawns are one of the areas which have greatly benefitted from the development of chemical weedkillers. Prior to their introduction, the only really successful method of controlling weeds was by hand-weeding. Imagine what a long and laborious job it would be, traversing your back garden on hands and knees, blunt kitchen knife in hand, digging and uprooting clumps of marauding dandelions, daisies and clover, and leaving in your wake unsightly bare holes— in which some broken roots would probably remain anyway. This would, of course, also be the most likely time to be surprised by an unexpected guest, or the vicar, probably creating the impression that one is a lunatic. How much better to spend a fraction of the time using a chemical preparation, achieving a much improved result, and even be caught unawares by such an aforementioned guest while relaxing in a sunlounger amid a beautiful sward, or casually playing croquet!

There is no one single way of achieving the perfect lawn, but by combining several methods, using the products now available, excellent results may be obtained. The aim is to remove all weeds with as little harm or disturbance to the existing grass as possible. Always buy the products which are specially formulated for use on lawns.

Selective Weedkiller

Selective weedkiller is almost magic in a bottle, but is based on a simple principle. It works as its name suggests by killing only certain types of growth, and is formulated to destroy all dicotyledon plants, i.e. the majority of weeds which grow in a lawn (see seedling references and note the pairs of cotyledons) while having no effect on monocotyledon grass. After application, the weed absorbs the chemical into its system; this stimulates its growth pattern to the point of being fatal, and subsequently the entire plant withers and dies. The grass growing nearby, finding less competition and more space, will soon fill its place.

The best time to apply a selective weedkiller is in early summer, before the weather gets too dry, and when both weeds and grass are growing vigorously. Ideally, choose a still, windless day, and thus avoid the danger of the weedkiller drifting on to other plants. *The rate of application and the dilution ratio with water are both very important, so do read the manufacturer's instructions very carefully and adhere strictly to them.* Apply evenly over the entire lawn area about 2 to 3 days after mowing, and do not re-mow for a further 3 days. This will deal with most of the weeds mentioned in this section, but a second application 4 to 6 weeks later may be necessary for the more persistent weeds which spread like chickweed and pearlwort.

Lawn Sand

This product preceded the selective weedkiller and works in a similar way. It is still available and is an effective, though often less complete method of weed control, but can have better effect on some weeds such as clover. It contains a mixture of sulphate of ammonia and sulphate of iron in sand, and selectively attacks the weeds and scorches off their top growth, turning them black. It may also temporarily discolour and brown the grass, too. The major disadvantage of this product is the overall discoloration, which is unsightly. However, this soon disappears and the grass benefits from the nitrogen content, which acts as a feed. It is ideal for shallow-rooted weeds like daisies, selfheal and many others, but has less long term effect on the deep-rooted varieties such as the dandelion. The advantages are that it comes ready prepared for use and does not involve dilution in water, its acid content diminishes some future weed growth, and the nitrogen element encourages the grass. It can also have some effect on moss.

Lawn sand needs both moisture and warmth for the best results. Apply in late spring, early in the morning when the dew is still on the grass, and the day promises to be fine, dry and warm. If no rain falls for 2 days after application, water lightly. Rake up all the dead foliage after 3 weeks, and apply a second application if necessary.

Chemical Gel or Spot Weedkiller

Whether selective weedkiller or lawn sand is used for the overall treatment of a lawn, there are still likely to be occasions when solitary, particularly tenacious weed specimens will re-appear. In such situations, chemical gel is the ideal solution to the problem. It can be applied directly on to the leaves of the offending weed with no danger to the grass in close proximity and, being a systemic weedkiller, will move throughout the plant's system and kill it entirely. As the weeds you are most likely to have to deal with by this method will be of the flat rosette or spreading type, like clover or a first year spear thistle, you may find that once the weed has been removed you are left with quite a large bare patch in its absence. This may be re-planted with grass seed, as the chemical has no adverse effect on the soil.

IMPORTANT—PLEASE NOTE

All the information given is intended to apply to established lawns. Specific mention should also be given to the situation of newly sown lawns or even newly sown areas in established lawns. Do not use *any* weedkiller other than ioxynil over a general area for at least six months after sowing. However, spot treatment can be used on individual weeds after they have reached the two leaf stage.

Weeds featured in this section:

Bulbous Buttercup
Cat's-ear
Common Bird's-foot-trefoil
Common Mouse-ear
Common Sorrel
Creeping Buttercup
Daisy
Field Wood-rush
Greater Plantain
Lesser Trefoil
Meadow Buttercup
Parsley-piert
Procumbent Pearlwort
Selfheal
Slender Speedwell
Smooth Hawk's-beard
White Clover
Yarrow
Yorkshire-fog

Moss

Bulbous Buttercup   *Ranunculus bulbosus*   Perennial

This buttercup has several characteristics by which it can be distinguished from the other members of its family. The Bulbous Buttercup has an erect, branched, hairy <u>stem with a</u> "bulb" at its base, thus giving it its name. The leaves have the family characteristic of being divided into three leaflets which are lobed and toothed, but differ in that they are hairy. The flowers are bright golden yellow and cup-shaped, but when open, the sepals (beneath petals) fold *back* against stalk.
n.b.: Does *not* have surface runners.

Height at maturity
6″–16″ (15–40 cm).

Stem
Erect, hairy and branched.

Flowers
Bright golden yellow and cup-shaped. When open, the sepals fold back against the stalk. Flowers May to August, generally starting before either the Creeping or Meadow Buttercup.

Leaves
Are divided into three leaflets which are lobed and further divided into broad-toothed segments. Differs from other buttercup varieties by being hairy.

Seedling

Cotyledons oval and pointed. True leaves long-stalked and lobed into trifoliate outline.

Chemical Treatment
Murphy Lawn Weedkiller or Tumbleweed Gel.

Bulbous Buttercup

Cat's-ear *Hypochoeris radicata* Perennial

Occurs as a flat, spreaded rosette of toothed, hairy leaves, from which grow erect, leafless stems, each bearing a single flat, yellow flower resembling a dandelion.

Height at maturity
9″–18″ (22–45 cm).

Stem
Erect, leafless and smooth. Hard to cut.

Flowers
Occur singly at the top of stems, are bright yellow and flat (approximately 1″ (2·5 cm) in diameter) and resemble a dandelion flower. They mature into downy seed-heads. Flowers June to September.

Leaves
Are oblong to lance-shaped, rough and hairy with deeply-toothed edges, and occur in spreaded rosettes.

Seedling

Cotyledons long and oval. True leaves pear-shaped with slightly-toothed margins.

Chemical Treatment
Murphy Lawn Weedkiller or Tumbleweed Gel.

Cat's-ear

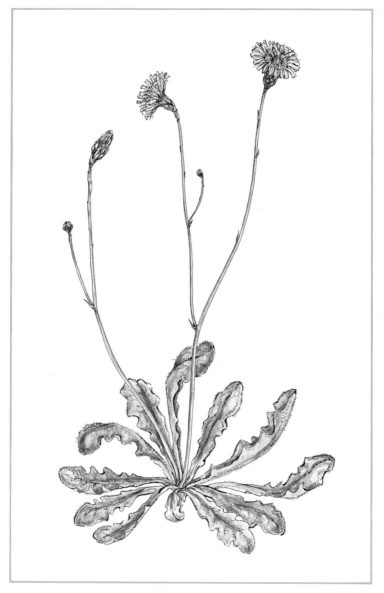

Common Bird's-foot-trefoil

Lotus corniculatus

Perennial

A prostrate, matted, rather pretty-looking plant, composed of many flat-lying stems which tend to curve upwards at the end. The leaves are trifoliate (divided into 3 leaflets) and are borne on short, thin stalks from the stem. Numerous clusters of approximately 5 or 6 bright yellowy-orange flowers occur in small groups at the top of long stalks. It has a deep tap root.

Height at maturity
Length of prostrate stems 4″–12″ (10–30 cm).

Stem
Long, thin, creeping and prostrate. At each leaf stalk joint with the stem grow two leaf-like stipules.

Flowers
Bright yellowy-orange and are often tinged with red or have a red stripe. They occur prolifically in clusters of 5 or 6 flower-heads in a small group at the end of a long stalk (although the number of flower-heads can vary from 2–10). When the flowers start to die they become a deeper orange colour. Flowers May to August.

Leaves
Are trifoliate, consisting of three oval, very slightly hairy leaflets, borne on a short, thin stalk from the stem, with two small stipules at the joint.

Seedling

Cotyledons small, oblong to oval-shaped. The true leaf is slightly hairy, trifoliate and long-stalked.

Chemical Treatment
Murphy Lawn Weedkiller in June and July, or Tumbleweed Gel.

Common Bird's-foot-trefoil

Common Mouse-ear
Cerastium holosteoides   Perennial

Other common name: Mouse-ear chickweed

A flat, "mat"-like plant, which sends out straggling, semi-erect, flowering stems which root at the nodes. It has small, hairy, lance-shaped leaves and spasmodic clusters of small white flowers. The whole plant has a rather "downy" appearance.

Height at maturity
3"–12" (8–30 cm) but mainly flat spreading.

Stem
Slender and straggling—can be 6"–12" (15–30 cm) long, round and hairy.

Flowers
Occur in clusters at top of stems, small and white on short stalks. Flowers April to September.

Leaves
Small, lance-shaped, hairy and stalkless, and grow in pairs along the stems.

Seedling

Cotyledons oval and pointed. True leaves similar, but rounder and hairy. The whole seedling is very small, dull dark green and has conspicuous, erect hairs.

Chemical Treatment
Murphy Lawn Weedkiller. Two applications recommended, 4 to 6 weeks apart.

Common Mouse-ear

Common Sorrel *Rumex acetosa*   Perennial

Other common name: Sour dock

A tallish, rather sparse-looking plant, with its thin, upright stems and sprays of reddish-pink flowers and seed pods. The leaves are few but distinctive in appearance, being quite shiny, and oval- to arrow-shaped with sharp-pointed basal lobes—rather like crab pincers.

Height at maturity
12″–36″ (30–90 cm) but kept to a rosette by mowing.

Stem
Upright, slender and grooved.

Flowers
Occur in close sprays of small, reddish-pink flowers and then seed pods. Flowers May to August.

Leaves
Shiny, oval or sometimes arrow-shaped with sharp-pointed basal lobes. Lower leaves long-stalked, upper leaves stalkless and clasp stem.

Seedling

Cotyledons oval-shaped. The first true leaf is round, but later leaves are spade-shaped with pointed basal lobes, more characteristic of the mature plant.

Chemical Treatment
Murphy Lawn Weedkiller or Tumbleweed Gel.

Common Sorrel

Creeping Buttercup *Ranunculus repens* Perennial

This is most easily distinguished from the other members of its family by its flat, spreaded appearance, and long, creeping, hairy stems which run overground and root at the nodes (joints). It has the usual bright, shiny yellow, cup-shaped flowers. It grows from long, stout roots.

Height at maturity
6″–12″ (15–30 cm). Prostrate runners can be up to 24″ (60 cm) long.

Stem
Has two types of stems. The overground runners, or stolons, which are tough and root at the nodes, and the upright flowering stems which are slender, branched and hairy.

Flowers
Are cup-shaped, bright golden yellow, and very shiny. The sepals (under petals) stand out from the stalk and this is a point which helps identify it from the Bulbous Buttercup where they fold back. Flowers May to August.

Leaves
The leaves are divided into three leaflets which are overall oval in outline, dark green, lobed, toothed, and slightly hairy. The stem leaves appear as if cut into ribbon-like segments.

Seedling

Cotyledons large, oval to round, and long-stalked. True leaves lobed into distinctive buttercup trifoliate leaf shape.

Chemical Treatment
Murphy Lawn Weedkiller or Tumbleweed Gel.

Creeping Buttercup

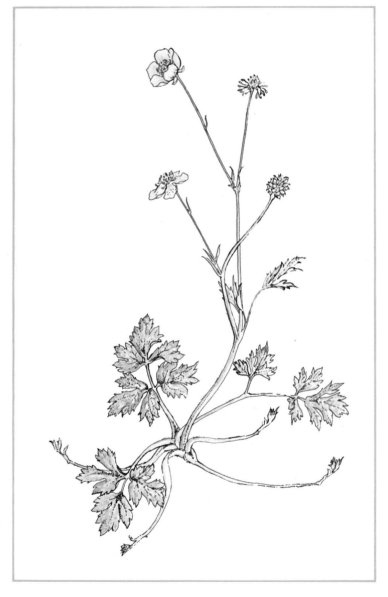

Daisy *Bellis perennis* Perennial

Needs little introduction—as there can be few of us who did not spend many a happy hour making daisy chains in our childhood. However, for identification purposes, occurs as a rosette of small, roundish leaves from which grow numerous slender, hairy stalks, each bearing a small white flower with a bright yellow centre.

Height at maturity
2″–6″ (5–15 cm).

Stem
Slender, hairy and leafless.

Flowers
Occur singly at top of stalks, and consist of numerous white, or pinkish-white florets with a bright yellow centre. The flowers close at sundown. Flowers all year round, but mainly March to November.

Leaves
Oval to round in shape, and quite thick, they have bluntly-toothed edges and are short-stalked. Occur in spreading rosettes.

Seedling

Cotyledons round. True leaves oval, long-stalked and hairy.

Chemical Treatment
Murphy Lawn Weedkiller or Tumbleweed Gel.

Daisy

Field Wood-rush
Luzula campestris   Perennial

An easily overlooked, tufted, grass-like weed, which can only be readily indentified during its short flowering period. It is composed of loose tufts of narrow, blade-like leaves which are often fringed with long, white hairs, and during flowering has thin, erect stems bearing clusters of chestnut brown flowers.

Height at maturity
4″–12″ (10–30 cm).

Stem
Erect, round and smooth, varying greatly in length.

Flowers
Occur in clusters at the top of each stem. Are a rich chestnut brown colour with light, shiny or transparent edges. Flowers April and May.

Leaves
Resemble grass blades—are long and narrow, with long white hairs and grow in loose tufts. These spread into a layered rosette, rather like the top of a pineapple.

Seedling
Appears as small version of the mature plant.

Chemical Treatment
Tumbleweed Gel (or kill whole infested area with Tumbleweed and re-sow).

Field Wood-rush

Greater Plantain   *Plantago major*   Perennial

A very common plant, easily recognised by its flat rosette of thick, broadly oval, ribbed leaves and tall stems culminating in spikes of greenish-brown flowers.

Height at maturity
4″–12″ (10–30 cm).

Stem
Upright, smooth and tough, with long spikes of greenish flowers.

Flowers
Occur in long spikes of densely clustered, minute, greenish-brown flowers with lilac-coloured anthers, at the top of upright stems. Flowers May to September.

Leaves
Are broadly oval in shape, thick, and have a distinctive ribbing on them. Attached by a long, thick stalk, they form a flat rosette. Can be smooth or slightly downy.

Seedling

Cotyledons long and narrow. True leaves oval and pointed with definite centre vein. Subsequent pairs of leaves are more distinguishable by their wavy edges and characteristic veining. The hypocotyl is usually purple, and the whole seedling tends to have a purple tinge.

Chemical Treatment
Murphy Lawn Weedkiller or Tumbleweed Gel.

Greater Plantain

Lesser Trefoil

Trifolium dubium   Annual

Other common name: Lesser yellow trefoil

Another member of the clover family, bearing some marked characteristics of the White Clover, but with an overall more delicate appearance. It has slender, spreading stems, with a small, round, yellow flower-head growing on a thin stalk from each leaf axil. These flowers turn pale brown. The characteristic trifoliate leaf grows at the base of each flower stalk.

Height at maturity
Prostrate, but each stem is 2″–10″ (5–25 cm) long.

Stem
Slender, spreading and prostrate.

Flowers
A flower-head, composed of numerous individual florets, occurs on a long, thin stalk at each leaf axil. The flowers are small, round and initially bright yellow, maturing to a light brown colour.

Leaves
Each leaf is composed of three leaflets, each one pear-shaped and ribbed. A single leaf occurs at each leaf axil along the length of the stem.

Seedling

Cotyledons long and oval. The shape of the two true leaves differs. One is apple-shaped, the other bears the characteristic trifoliate pattern. Both are very long-stalked.

Chemical Treatment
Murphy Lawn Weedkiller in June and July.

Lesser Trefoil

Meadow Buttercup *Ranunculus acris* Perennial

Very much taller than either the Creeping or Bulbous Buttercup, it has slender, erect stems, bright yellow, saucer-shaped flowers, and long-stalked leaves which, while retaining the characteristic buttercup appearance, are sometimes divided into 5 or 7 lobes.

Height at maturity
12″–40″ (30–100 cm).

Stem
Erect, slender and branched. Hairless.

Flowers
Bright yellow, and more saucer than cup-shaped. The sepals (under petals) are not reflexed. Flowers April to September.

Leaves
Divided into 3, 5 or even 7 leaflets which are deeply lobed and raggedly toothed.

Seedling

Cotyledons round to oval and stalked. True leaves characteristically lobed and hairy, with long stalks.

Chemical Treatment
Murphy Lawn Weedkiller or Tumbleweed Gel.

Meadow Buttercup

Parsley-piert *Aphanes arvensis* Annual

A small, spreading plant, which can quickly cover large areas of ground like a mat. Has distinctive fan-shaped leaves which occur in clumps on short flowering stalks off the main prostrate stem. The small, green, seed-like flowers occur in dense clusters in the leaf axils.

n.b.: This plant flowers and re-seeds at a very immature stage, therefore creating large colonies in a short period.

Height at maturity
1″–6″ (2·5–15 cm).

Stems
Prostrate, branched and hairy.

Flowers
Clusters of pale green, seed-like flowers occur in the leaf axils. Flowers April to September.

Leaves
Overall fan-shaped in outline with a short stalk. Each leaf is divided—or lobed—into three segments, which are further deeply toothed.

Seedling

Cotyledons round. True leaves lobed, one is again larger than its partner. The whole seedling is very small and a bright blue-green colour.

Chemical Treatment
Murphy Lawn Weedkiller or Tumbleweed Gel.

Parsley-piert

Procumbent Pearlwort   *Sagina procumbens* Perennial

A tiny, tufted plant, composed of a central dense rosette of narrow leaves from which spread long, prostrate stems. These stems in turn have tufts of tiny, thin leaves at intervals along them, and from each tuft springs a thin stalk bearing a single, tiny, white flower. When out of flower it can easily be mistaken for a moss.

Height at maturity
Prostrate stems 1″–4″ (2·5–10 cm) long.

Stem
Prostrate, roots at the nodes, and has several tufts of tiny linear leaves along its length.

Flowers
Occur singly on thin stalks from each tuft of leaves along stem. Are tiny and white, composed of 4 petals, although these are often absent, leaving only the 4 green sepals remaining. Flowers May to September.

Leaves
Occur first as a central rosette of thin, dark, and shiny pointed leaves, then as tufts along stem.

Seedling
Does not appear as a characteristic seedling, but more as a small tuft of grass with narrow leaves.

Chemical Treatment
Murphy Lawn Weedkiller. Two sprays 4 to 6 weeks apart.

Procumbent Pearlwort

Selfheal   *Prunella vulgaris*   Perennial

A compact, spreading plant, its stems send up square, erect, flowering stems bearing clusters of bright purple flowers. Each cluster of flowers always has a pair of pointed, stalkless leaves beneath it. The lower leaves are stalked, pointed and downy.

Height at maturity
Upright stems 2″ (5 cm), prostrate length 12″ (30 cm).

Stems
Creeping and prostrate, but sending up square, erect, flowering stems of varying lengths. Both are very slightly hairy.

Flowers
Occur in thick, tubular clusters of tiny, bright purple flowers. These flower-heads or clusters always have a pair of pointed leaves immediately below them. Flowers June to October.

Leaves
Oval and pointed in shape, and slightly downy. They always grow in pairs and occur in intermittent groups along the stem. The stem leaves are stalkless, the lower leaves stalked.

Seedling

Cotyledons long-stalked, spade-shaped with indented top and pointed basal lobes. True leaves are long-stalked, veined, and have irregular margins.

Chemical Treatment
Murphy Lawn Weedkiller or Tumbleweed Gel.

Selfheal

Slender Speedwell *Veronica filiformis* Perennial

Other common name: Creeping speedwell

A delicate-looking, but deceptively troublesome plant. Has tiny kidney-shaped leaves, and fragile-looking, blue-mauve flowers on thread-like stalks. Creeps and spreads rapidly, rooting at the nodes and forming large patches.

n.b.: This weed is particularly troublesome in lawns, where if cut by a mower and discarded by it, the cutting merely re-roots itself—thus such mowings should be collected and burnt.

Height at maturity
Prostrate. Stems vary greatly, but can creep and grow to a considerable length.

Stems
Very slender and weak.

Flowers
Individual, tiny, blue-mauve flowers grow at the end of long, thread-like stalks from the stem. Flowers in April and May.

Leaves
Small, round to kidney-shaped with softly-toothed edges and short-stalked. Occur alternately up stem, or in pairs.

Seedling
Seeds are very rarely set in Britain. Vegetative reproduction.

Chemical Treatment
Mortegg, or ioxynil-containing selective weedkiller.

Slender Speedwell

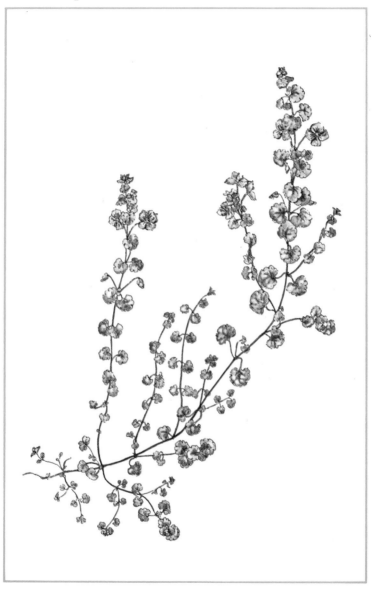

Smooth Hawk's-beard
Crepis capillaris

Annual or Biennial

A straggly-looking plant. Composed of a basal rosette of thin, toothed leaves; tall, slender, branched stems, which have narrow, jagged, sharply-pointed leaves clasping them, and ultimately loose clusters of small, yellow, daisy-like flowers.
n.b.: There are 8 species of Hawk's-beard in this country, all very similar in their characteristics, but Smooth Hawk's-beard is the most widespread.

Height at maturity
6″–36″ (15–90 cm).

Stem
Upright, branched, slender and furrowed.

Flowers
Small (1 to 1·3 cm in diameter), bright yellow, and composed of numerous florets. These are first encased in goblet-shaped involucres. Occur in pairs at top of stems, and mature into downy, white seed heads. Flowers June to September.

Leaves
Base leaves are long, thin, and raggedly toothed, forming a rosette. The stem leaves are smaller, but very pointed at the top and also at the base where they clasp the stem—they are overall arrow-shaped with jagged edges. Can be hairy or smooth.

Seedling

Cotyledons oval. The true leaves are irregularly and slightly toothed, and hairy.

Chemical Treatment
Murphy Lawn Weedkiller or Tumbleweed Gel.

Smooth Hawk's-beard

White Clover   *Trifolium repens*   Perennial
Other common name: Dutch clover

An endearing if troublesome plant! Easily recognised by its distinctive trifoliate leaves and sweet-smelling, white, many-floreted flower-heads. Again, there can be few of us who have not spent many a childhood hour examining this weed in the greatest detail in the search for a rare "lucky" four-leafed specimen! However, it is generally unpopular in the garden due to its vigorous creeping, rooting stems and ability to spread rapidly across the ground or lawn, creating vast, clumped masses. Although clover on lawns stays green under drought conditions, the patches are very slippery when wet.

Height at maturity 3″–12″ (8–30 cm).

Stem Overground runners root at the nodes, sending up erect, slender leaf or flower stalks, bearing a single leaf or flower-head.

Flowers The flower-heads occur singly at the top of a slender stem, are white or tinged with pink, delicately perfumed and composed of many individual florets, forming a dense, round ball. As each flower fades, it withers and droops. Are highly attractive to bees. Flowers May to October.

Leaves Each leaf occurs singly at top of a slender stem, and is composed of three individual round leaflets. These are dark green and have a distinct white band across each one of them.

Seedling

 Cotyledons are a flat oval-shape. The true leaves are long-stalked, hairless, and differ in shape. One is kidney-shaped, the other divided into the characteristic three leaflets. Both often have white marks at the base.

Chemical Treatment
Murphy Lawn Weedkiller in June and July. Or kill off infested area with Tumbleweed and re-sow.

White Clover

Yarrow   *Achillea millefolium*   Perennial

Other common name: Milfoil

An erect plant, with long, narrow leaves which are divided into many finely-toothed segments, giving them a feathery appearance, and flat clusters of small, creamy-white or pinkish-white flowers at top of stems. Has a very strong, but not unpleasant, smell.

Height at maturity
12″–24″ (30–60 cm).

Stem
Upright, grooved and a dull grey-green colour. Covered with soft hairs.

Flowers
Occur in flat clusters of numerous, small, creamy-white, or pinkish-white flowers at top of stems. Flowers June to October.

Leaves
Overall long and narrow in shape with a feathery appearance. Each leaf is divided into many finely-toothed segments. The lower leaves are stalked, upper leaves stalkless.

Seedling

Cotyledons round to pear-shaped. True leaves are very hairy and have sharply-pointed teeth.

Chemical Treatment
Murphy Lawn Weedkiller.

Yarrow

Yorkshire-fog   *Holcus lanatus*   Perennial

A grass weed, it consists of a clump of stems, each of which grows directly from the root. The stems bear narrow, pointed, and softly hairy leaves which sheath the stem at their bases. The stem tapers as each leaf unfurls, ending in a very thin, erect stem bearing a feathery flower-head, composed of numerous greenish-purple spikelets.

Height at maturity
8″–24″ (20–60 cm).

Stem
Tall, erect and tapered. Is covered for much of its length by the downy leaf sheaths.

Flowers
Are pale green, pink or greenish-purple, and occur in spiked clusters at top of stem. Flowers May to August.

Leaves
Long, thin, and blade-like, with a sheath around the stem which unfurls singly at each node. Are soft and downy, both in appearance and to the touch. The lower leaf sheaths often have red veins.

Seedling
Appears as small version of mature plant.

Chemical Treatment
Tumbleweed Gel. If intensive infestation, kill off affected area with Tumbleweed, and re-sow.

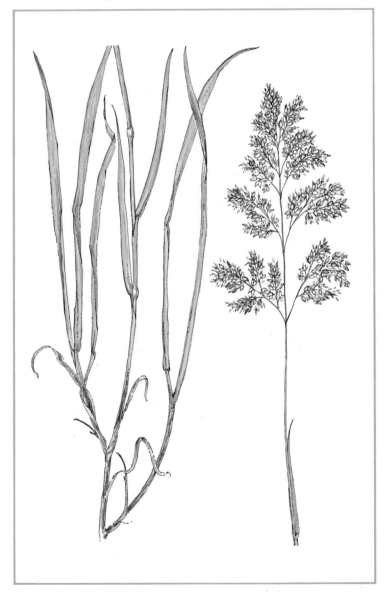

Moss comes in a category of its own. Its growth is perpetuated mainly by the presence of excessive water, i.e. a poorly-drained area of lawn, soil compactation or an area often in deep shade. (This is substantiated by the fact that moss grows profusely during wet periods but dries up and dies away in the summer heat). Over-acidity in the soil or infertility are also common reasons, as they produce bare patches which is an open invitation for moss, and once it is established, it reproduces abundantly both by vegetative means and spores. Moss is not affected by any selective weedkillers, so a specialised proprietary brand of moss killer should be applied. The dead moss should then be raked out of the lawn and a complete fertilizer applied. However, for long-lasting effect, the best method of control is to discover the basic reason for the presence of moss and to rectify that problem, be it drainage, soil deficiency or aeration.

Chemical Treatment
Super Moss Killer

Section 4 - Weeds in paths, drives and patios

Weeds in paths are unsightly, slippery and therefore dangerous. After a shower of rain a walk from a front door to garden gate down a neglected, weed-overgrown path can be as dangerous as crossing a busy road.

Any of the weeds mentioned in the first two sections of this book can be found in these concreted or shingled areas. Perennial weeds can grow from roots or stems under paving stones or tarmac; open, shingle-type areas attract the seeding annuals. Fortunately, treatment is relatively simple, as these are basically non-growing areas—in terms of cherished plants—so the application of weedkillers can be more widespread and general. For the best, long-lasting results, application should be carried out in two stages. First by using an overall application of a *translocated weedkiller*, e.g. Tumbleweed, to remove all existing weeds and kill them entirely, right through to the roots. Follow this one week later by applying an overall application of a *residual weedkiller*, e.g. Weedex—this will keep your path or drive area free from future weeds for up to twelve months, as it remains in the top 2″ (5 cm) of ground, and kills any new weeds as they germinate. Alternatively, apply a combined translocated and residual weedkiller product, e.g. Super Weedex.

A few precautions should be observed before applying a residual weedkiller:

1. Do not use it under trees, shrubs or any land intended for future planting within the twelve-month period.

2. Do not use it on any sloping concrete or tarmac drives where rain could wash a dilution down on to flower beds or plants.

3. Do remember the roots of any trees or shrubs which may extend under a pathway and *do not apply* in that area. However, this weedkiller does not creep sideways so it may be used right up to the edges of lawns and flowerbeds.

4. It will not kill moss.

Section 5 - Weeds in fruit gardens

Fruit growing is another area of gardening where one's emotions run high. The idea of growing seemingly inexhaustible supplies of plump, luscious fruit in one's own domain, and thus being able to pluck and eat it at peak condition is indeed an appealing one. In reality it has its problems. In my experience, birds and slugs always seem to beat me to this ideal, however that is a problem on which I can offer little advice! The other blight of fruit growing is again the weed brigade. Being another area which attracts little attention from the gardener other than at pruning and harvesting times, it presents an ideal situation for weeds to amass. However, with relatively little effort and time, these weeds can be abated.

Once the bushes, canes or trees have been established at least 12 months, the surrounding soil can be treated with a selective residual weedkiller, thus rendering the ground weed-free for the entire season. This should be applied to moist, weed-free soil in the spring following a carefully applied application of translocated weedkiller to remove existing perennial weeds.

With younger trees, etc, it is likely that you will be planting these yourself. Prepare the ground well first before planting, and hoe up any annual weeds as they appear and spot treat the perennial weeds. After the first year you will be able to treat the surrounds with the residual weedkiller.

To get your fruit garden weed-free is a worthwhile long-term project. Your fruit bushes and trees will be with you for many years, and once you have commenced weed treatment, and if you continue with it annually, the results you achieve will improve and be more effective as each year passes.

A final note on weed habitat

I would finally like to mention that although within this book I have divided the garden into four basic areas, namely cultivated ground, herbaceous borders, pathways and lawns, and have included in each section the weeds *most likely* to be found, every garden is different, and weeds are by nature wayward, nomadic creatures. This makes it difficult to state precisely where they may decide to grow.

In some cases these areas overlap, and it is quite likely that some weeds included in one section could easily be prolific in another.

Therefore, virtually any of the weeds detailed could be found in any of the four basic garden areas, but of course the tall-growing perennial weeds are unlikely to flourish on well used pathways or on well mown lawns.

I think it is also an interesting fact that the soil type of your particular garden can be identified by analysing which weeds grow in it, where, and with what profusion. There are books available which explore the subject of soil in detail, its composition, type, merit and weaknesses. This may or may not interest you, however it could explain why, if you have difficulty in growing a particular type of flower or plant in your garden, Aunt Flo can do so living elsewhere—it's not necessarily her green fingers!

Glossary

Alternate Descriptive of the leaf arrangement along a stem where the leaves grow singly, but each leaf grows on the opposite side of the stem to the previous leaf.

Annual A plant completing its life cycle within one year.

Axil The angle formed where a leaf or leaf stalk meets the main stem.

Axis Central point of inflorescence or other whorl of growth.

Biennial A plant completing its life cycle within two years, feeding and growing during the first year and flowering or fruiting in the second year.

Basal At the base or bottom.

Bract A type of leaf which grows beneath a flower or flower cluster.

Bulbil A small reproductive bulb which occurs above ground.

Cotyledons The first two leaves of a plant which appear after germination of its seed. (Only one cotyledon in the case of grasses).

Dicotyledon Flowering plant with two cotyledons.

Disk Florets Tube-like flowers at the centre of a flower-head.

Downy Covered with short, weak, soft hairs.

Floret A small individual flower head which usually forms part of a composite flower.

Hypocotyl The length of stem between soil surface and cotyledonary node.

Inflorescence Collection and arrangement of flower-heads and stalks.

Involucre A collection of bracts interlocked together which surround a flower-head.

Leaflet One division of a compound leaf, usually similar in appearance to the main leaf.

Linear Long and narrow with parallel sides.

Lobe Deeply divided segment of a leaf, but not actually separated from it.

Margin Edge of leaf.

Mealy Appearing as if covered with flour.

Monocotyledon Plant which produces one cotyledon only.

Node Point on a stem at which one or more leaves arise. Often appears as a slightly swollen bump.

Opposite Where two leaves rise from the same point, but on opposite sides of a stem.

Perennial A plant which lives several years and usually flowers each year once established.

Pinnate A regular arrangement of leaflets on each side of a common stalk, giving the appearance of a feather.

Prostrate Lying closely along the surface of the ground.

Ray Florets Outer ring of petals, larger and more "showy" than inner disk florets.

Rhizome Creeping underground stem of perennial plant which sends up new shoots each season.

Rosette A flat, spreaded arrangement of leaves radiating outwards from a central point. The leaves usually overlap.

Sepals The outer segments of a flower.

Sheath Close fitting tubular tissue surrounding a stem.

Spike An elongated cluster of closely spaced, stalkless flowers.

Spikelet Small spike.

Spore "Seed" of some lower forms of plant life.

Stolon Horizontal stem spreading above, or just below, ground, which roots and produces new plant.

Stipule Small leaf-like appendage, occurring at base of leaf stalk.

Subtended Occurring below.

Trifoliate Having three leaflets.

True leaves Second pair of leaves occurring in a seedling, following the cotyledons.

Umbel Flower cluster branched like an umbrella, with all the stalks equal in length and arising from a single axis.

Whorl Arrangement of leaves in a circle around the stem.

Index